-NICOLE BROCX LEE'S-

From **Wedding Bells** To

Hand Grenades

WHAT ONE ARMY WIFE WISHED

HER CHURCH & COMMUNITY KNEW ABOUT

DEPLOYMENT & THE MILITARY FAMILY

But you are a chosen generation, a royal priesthood, a holy nation. His own special people, that you may proclaim the praises of Him who called you out of darkness and into His marvelous light.

1 Peter 2:9

A TRAITMARKER BOOK

www.traitMarker.com

-NICOLE BROCX LEE-

From **Wedding Bells** To

Hand Grenades

WHAT ONE ARMY WIFE WISHED
HER CHURCH & COMMUNITY KNEW ABOUT
DEPLOYMENT & THE MILITARY FAMILY

Dedication

*To my self-sacrificing husband, **Michael**...*

who has laid down his life in so many ways that most don't know, to protect the freedoms of this beautiful country that we live in, and the lives of those he serves with overseas, foreign and domestic. You are a humble hero and a true inspiration to many, including myself.

*To all of my sons: **Keir, Dane, Rainier** and **Theodore**...*

*You boys are the joys of my life, my companions, and my best friends. **Keir,** you are my wild bundle of adventure who is a one-man party in and of yourself. You follow after your dreams, no matter what others may say. You are my first-born treasure and will always be my Little Bear. **Dane,** you are my steadfast, solid, and responsible young man. I love to laugh with you and am so proud of you and your entire sweet family. You will always be my Bookie. **Rainier,** you are my Rainier. You are my seeker of truth, and I love to have deep, intellectual conversations with you about everything in life. Don't ever play Pictionary with us, because you and I know what the other one is drawing with one line! You excel at everything you do, but you will always be my baby. **Theo,** you are my sweet and tenderhearted teddy bear. You are so very musically gifted that it blows me away. You are determined and dedicated, and I am proud of all you've done so far at your young age. You will always be my Theodore bear cub. **All** of you boys are loving and caring young men, and I know for a fact that the world will continue to be impacted by all the lives you touch. I couldn't be more proud of all four of you.*

-CONTENTS-

There is minority group right in the the United States of America: approximately 2.3 million right now. Although they are spoken of and about frequently, this group the Christian church often overlooks as a *special-needs group.* No, I'm not talking about another race or nationality. Even though they comprise less than 1% of the entire U.S population of roughly 313 million, this group with their unique and complicated needs definitely needs to be reached and encouraged with the unconditional love and compassion of Jesus. This often-unreached people group is frequently referred to as the United States military.

My husband and I have been married for over 27 years, and he has been in the military for more than 22 years. When we married, Mike had recently enlisted in the Army and was frequently gone for weeks at a time during periods of deployment. Looking back, I realize that he was not really gone that often compared to what was to come. I'm grateful that Mike was home more often at the beginning of his military career as I was a new wife and quickly becoming a new mom. After three years and a 2-month-old son, we joined the civilian world.

When Mike left the military, we moved from Olympia, Washington to San Diego, California and began what we thought would be a normal life. Mike became a full-time student and had several civilian jobs that ranged from selling cars to waiting tables to being a park ranger, etc. During the short period that Mike was financially successful in car sales, he felt that God was directing him back into the military. My response was "No way are we going back into the military. I hate it!"

It took two more years before every option for making an income in the civilian world was blocked to us. Car sales plummeted for Mike, and he was making almost nothing financially. Even though the number of hours he worked were over the limit, we only qualified for a small amount of food stamps. In addition, we put the mortgage of our small townhouse on our credit cards until we had no credit limit left. In the middle of all of this, we had two more sons.

Oh, I loved San Diego so much! It took us getting into a terrible financial bind before I realized that going back into the military wasn't a bad option after all. I was so determined to live in my dream location that I became an obstacle for what seemed to be God's plan for Mike as a soldier and for my life as a military wife.

After getting knocked over the head financially with a ton of bricks and agreeing that the military was the best option for us, Mike went back into the military, back to Washington, and back to his old unit. This time I had a renewed fervor knowing that we were going back into the military, because it was apparent that it was what God wanted us to do. It wasn't just an occupation that seemed to be the last option.

Because I have been the wife of a soldier and of a civilian, I understand the polar differences between the two worlds. Be assured that civilian and military life are completely separate worlds.

As I write this, we have four sons aged 26, 22, 20 and 16. For the last 13 years my husband has been has been on 8 combat deployments (one before 9/11), totaling over 50 months in combat. During the time that he's at home, he has to train (and often out of state), keeping him from actually being home more than a few months at a time. All I can say is that there was nothing we could have done apart from relying on God to keep us together.

In this book I include the life stories from people with whom I have spoken and know very well. Although each military family is different, we all have common struggles and needs that are unique to the military lifestyle. So it's important that this book not be just my story but the story of a several military families. While we each have our own story, we can learn from each others' experiences. I am adding these clips of their lives, because I believe that their stories would be beneficial for others to hear. These accounts are from real people who have had unique experiences and trials due to the affects of military life. The names and locations of most of them have been changed to protect their privacy.

It's my belief that if the church were more aware of the normal issues of military families, it would be better able to help them. In writing as a military wife, I am not trying to exclude or diminish the life of the military husband or anyone else. I am only writing from experiences that are true to me and true to what I know. I hope that nothing in this book will offend anyone, because that isn't my intention. I just hope to bring to light the unique and often overwhelming needs of an often overlooked group of individuals and families.

I have also surveyed about 100 people in order to gather information from both the military wives' points of view and also the children (most of whom are now in their mid to upper 20's), particularly the ones who have had to endure the deployments of their dads.

I have had many women who are not in the military ask me *How do you do it? I could never do what you do with your husband in danger and gone all the time.* Well, if someone would have informed me when I first got married that this was the lifestyle I would be living, I'm not sure if I would have believed I could do it. Thankfully *I can do all things through Christ who strengthens me* (Philippians 4:13), because in my own strength there is no way I could have endured.

I began writing with goals and a vision of sorts. However, the book seems to have taken itself in its own hands and has evolved into something quite different than what I had first intended. I see this as a positive thing, though. From the time I began working on this book until the writing of this segment, I have grown and changed so much. Growth is a good thing, and stagnation can cause us to be rancid. I don't want a rancid life. Each experience I've been through, every wonderful person that I've met, and each place that I have visited has brought richness to my life when I have allowed for it.

My hope is that your eyes would be opened to all that is around you. This world is a beautiful place in so many ways.

Yes, there is much sorrow and destruction, and it is too easy to focus on the negative and be bogged down by our surroundings. Instead, let's take these experiences and allow them to enrich our lives. Let's take what we have gone through and allow the situations to be used to help others.

Last but not least, I want to point out that I am writing this from the viewpoint of an Army wife. Throughout the book I will refer to our husbands as *soldiers.* I am aware that Navy, Marines, Air Force and Coast Guard personnel are referred to by different terms. I'm not excluding the other branches of service, but I live the life of an Army wife and am more familiar with Army lingo. So anytime I use the word *soldier,* I'm including all branches of service. Also, I know that many female soldiers deploy, leaving their husbands and children behind, too. I'm including them as well!

- CHAPTER 1 -

The Life of a Missionary Family- Would That Be You?

We are therefore Christ's ambassadors,
as though God were making His appeal through us.
2 Corinthians 5:20a

What does it mean to be an ambassador? Several definitions are available in the dictionary: *a special representative; an official agent on a special mission; the highest-ranking representative appointed by one country or government to represent it in another.*

If we combine these definitions, it summarizes the kind of life that God wants us to live. As Christians, we are special representatives who have been sent out on a unique mission to represent Christ. All Christians have this calling. As a military family, it is an honor literally to be ambassadors for Christ and sent out to various locations and countries. This is true for the family as a whole, and it is also true for the husband (or wife) as he is deployed. This is an honor that we should never take lightly. It's imperative that we see ourselves as ambassadors.

So what does it mean to be a military spouse and to have a military family? Is the military just a profession where we put in our time, get a paycheck, and live our lives? If that were the case, then any job would be sufficient to accomplish those tasks, wouldn't it? We ought to realize that being in the military is a calling from God of the most fundamental sort. Our family is a missionary family. Yes, *missionary.* The dictionary defines the word missionary as *one who is sent on a mission, especially one sent to do religious or charitable work in a territory or foreign land.* We may not be sent out by a church or a religious organization, but we are sent out by the military and, ultimately, we are sent out by God.

Missionary Family

Yes, in a real way we are called by being sent to other locations around the nation and to other countries around the world. Matthew 28:19-20 says *Therefore go and make disciples of all nations, baptizing them in the name of the Father and the Son and of the Holy Spirit and teaching them to obey everything I have commanded you. And surely I am with you always, to the end of the age.* One of the most difficult aspects of being in the military is the frequent moves. This entails being uprooted from all of which we are familiar (family, friends, location) and being placed somewhere that is often not of our choice. I have to remember that I am a missionary and that I may never feel completely at home where I am. Thankfully, where we live now has really seemed to be an oasis for our family in so many ways. Although Mike's current job still takes him away from the family on trips with the military, he is not deploying overseas now. The amount of time that he is gone is so much shorter than it was when we lived in Tennessee. I am very thankful for this hiatus in his military career.

Being a missionary family is not an easy task. When going through all the years of deployments, I often had to remind myself that we were there for one reason and one purpose. Yes, Uncle Sam gave us orders, but Romans 8:28 says that *God works for the good of those who love Him, who have been called according to His purpose.* Notice it says *His* purpose and not *our* purpose. Only God can see the whole picture. We see just a glimpse. Being a military spouse means that I signed up for a life of adventure, and one part of that adventure can be frequent moves to distant locations in various climates and settings. I try to find what I like in each location and realize that I probably won't be living there for too long anyway (so I might as well enjoy it).

As we struggle through the ups and downs of our lives as military wives, we often forget what our purpose is here on the earth as Christians. Our job is to glorify God: to demonstrate the highest quality of love and commitment, especially when it's not the easiest thing to do. It's not primarily to be comfortable or happy or even content. We are not here to live an easy life, but we are here to live the life to which God has called us. He never said it would be easy. But He does say in many several places that He will be here with us. Matthew 28:20 reminds us that *Surely I am with you always, to the end of the age.* We can be assured that when times seem too difficult to bear, we can recall God's promises and specifically know that He will always be with us. Even though we are not always happy with our situation, we can retain a joy that is not based on physical circumstances or pure emotion. Our joy revolves around the true peace when we know we are following God's will.

So many people in the Bible have had to move because the Lord called them to a specific location. When I look at my life and feel the urge to complain during my relocation situations, it helps me to remember what so many of these great heroes in the Bible had to endure. I think about Ruth and how she made the choice to move out of her homeland to the land of her mother-in-law, Naomi. Not only did she make a new home in a foreign land, but she was a help to Naomi by working for her and also by giving her a grandchild. This grandchild eventually became grandfather to King David.

In my life I have countless times felt that we moved to our specific location for purposes that weren't simply random. I'm currently going through a box that I've had in my garage full of those odds-and-ends that I didn't want to throw away but wasn't sure where to put them. It was finally time to go through that box. In the box I found several letters and pictures of many people we had met through the years who we would never have met were we not in the military and lived where we hadn't been assigned. In several of these letters there are people writing who had been blessed by how we came into their lives and helped them in so many ways. This was seriously encouraging and uplifting to me, and I am thankful that I didn't throw these letters away earlier.

Many things like these letters of encouragement keep me on track and remind me just how our family clearly is a missionary family. I also found letters to my sons, from my sons, and about my sons in this box. It is so exciting to see that my husband is not the only missionary in the family but that we all are missionaries as a family unit.

David is a father who has been in the military for over 20 years. He had considered getting out of the military and becoming a pastor because he felt the call to be a vocational minister. Then it hit him that he is already one *while* being a soldier: just without the title of *pastor.* David puts it simply:

I think as Christians, we should all consider ourselves missionaries. God says to make disciples. I believe this applies to all of us all the time. We must be faithful with what He has given us, no matter how small or large.

Christians must understand their role as missionaries. If we can appreciate this role, we know that as a Christian soldier or spouse of a soldier we are spreading God's light wherever we are sent. *You are the light of the world. A city on a hill cannot be hidden. Neither do people light a lamp and put it under a bowl. Instead they put it in its stand, and it gives light to everyone in the house. In the same way, let your light shine before men, that they may see your good deeds and praise your Father in heaven.* (Matthew 5:14-16)

My husband should be a light as a soldier. *Being a light* means to stand out from others by being a good example and to show people what true love really is *in actionable ways.* I should do the same as a wife. Our marriage should be an example to others looking for how to live in this often difficult world. I should be a light as his wife. And our marriage should be a light and an example to others who are looking for this kind of hope. As a Christian in the military (as with anywhere else) we will be scrutinized in everything we do. While we are not expected to be perfect, we do need to realize that people look to us for hope and probably more than they look to others.

Tips from Chapter 1

• Identify a few Bible verses to memorize that help put into perspective your specific purpose as a military wife and ambassador. Do the same with your children.

- If you find it too cliché or unreasonable to see yourself ambassador, read up on ambassadors and their families. Find out what kinds of things ambassadors do & what lifestyles their families lead. Note similarities between your life and theirs.

- Read books on the lives of missionaries and/or watch documentaries and note the similarities of the lives your family lives.

- Write an encouraging letter to a military family or spouse. If you live in a foreign country, find out who the American ambassador to that country is & write them a letter. This will mean so much more to them than you know.

Questions from Chapter 1

- What pressures do you feel as a military wife? Do you feel that you have to be happier than you feel for the sake of others? Do you feel that you are losing your identity as a person first and foremost? Do you feel like your personal interests and concerns don't matter in light of your husband's job?

- Do you feel like you are being a genuine example to others right where you are living? If not, in what ways can you be a genuine example without having to stretch your personality farther than it should go.

- What does your personal, private attitude look like in actions to those around you?

- If you look at the life of someone like Ruth in the Bible, how do you see ways that you could relate to her lifestyle changes before, during, and after her move?

- Who are some other people in the Bible who had to move because God told them to? What were their struggles? How did this benefit them?

POINTS YOU WANT TO REMEMBER

feel free to jot down notes below...

- C H A P T E R 2 -

Your Husband-Soldier: Be His Biggest Fan

Who can find a virtuous wife? For her worth is far above rubies.
The heart of her husband safely trusts her; so he will have no lack of
gain. She does him good and not evil all the days of her life.

Proverbs 31: 10-12

Being the wife of a military man is *one* of the most important
and difficult jobs imaginable, and it's imperative to understand
the impact we have on our spouse that will determine his
success as a soldier. A wife should support her husband with her
words and her actions. Either I can be his #1 fan, or I can be (or
contribute to) his downfall. The choice is up to me.

Can you remember when you were going through a difficult
time and how a kind word was so encouraging? Think about the
flip side. Do you remember a time when you were so
discouraged that one harsh word made the situation seemed
overwhelming and hopeless?

A husband needs to know that his wife supports who he is,
what he does, and what he stands for. You may be thinking
Surely I can't make that big of a difference by my actions and
words. A man's success should be completely up to him: how he
reacts, how he advances in his job, and how he does in his
career. The Bible, however, describes the power of the words
we speak. *The tongue has the power of life and death.* Proverbs
18:21a and *With the tongue we praise our Lord and Father, and*
with it we curse men, who have been made in God's likeness.
Out of the same mouth come praise and cursing. My brothers,
this should not be. James 3:9-10

I am not with Mike when he is at work, but he takes a part of me with him wherever he goes. I know my husband better than anyone else, so I need to build him up and speak lovingly to him *in a way that he understands.*I can't assume that the things that make me feel loved and cared for are the same for him.

Several good books on the market can help wives determine what actions positively affects their husbands. One highly recommended book is *The Five Love Languages* by Gary Chapman. When my husband and I had been married for 12 years, we experienced a stressful time when I felt like my needs were not getting met. But Mike *really* believed he was doing all he could to make me happy. One of the pastors in our church told Mike about *The Five Love Languages*. We both read it and were enlightened. It was such a breakthrough in our communication which we always had considered excellent. As a wife, I can never learn too much about my spouse. So anything I do to improve our marriage will enrich our lives as a unit and improve my husband's role as a soldier.

I must always remember that I am my husband's main support team and fan club. I must encourage him consistently, because the military life is not one where he will be necessarily encouraged morally. He's often thrown into a system that often looks down on anything morally sound. I need to realize the importance of being there for him in word, praying for him daily, and letting him know that he is, indeed, *my* hero. A verse that addresses this is 1 Thessalonians 5:11: *Therefore encourage one another and build each other up, just as in fact you are doing.* Always, *always* encourage!

Our husbands are heroes, and they need to hear that from us *more* than anyone else. No matter what our husbands' jobs are, they are protecting and defending our country to keep the freedoms of which we are often oblivious and that we often take for granted. Whether our husbands are battling with real weapons or are cooks or janitors, their jobs are vital to our country. Wives consider the big picture of what our men are doing. *We* must help them to realize its importance.

We cannot assume that our husbands know how we feel. They must hear these words from us. Because our husbands are often gone on deployments and trainings, it's that much more important to go out of our way to do those seemingly trivial things that mean a lot. *Words of affirmation* is one of my husband's main love languages. I grew up in a family that was more sarcastic and quick-witted. I have to remember to hold my tongue, because it's my nature to say something that I think would be funny but in reality is insensitive or hurtful to my husband. Humor gets lost in translation even more because we are away from each other so much and we really don't have those spare moments for him to adjust incrementally to my sarcasm. It's just as easy for me to think of kind words to say that build him up, and it's definitely more beneficial to our marriage.

My friend, Stephanie (whose husband was with mine on two deployments) knows what a true warrior and hero is. She says:

While I feel sympathy every time I hear of a celebrity dying, I just can't understand how big of a deal they make it when they pass away. They were 'heroes' and 'idols.' They make front-page news. Sad that when a soldier, a REAL hero dies, fighting for their country, it rarely (if ever) makes the front page. Those are the heroes people should mourn, the ones who make the ultimate sacrifice, not some drug addicted celebrity.

If we consider our husbands to be our heroes, then what are some specific things that we can do to encourage and build them up? The *first* thing is to know what my husband's specific job is as a soldier. If the husband is a Christian, his primary job as a soldier is to be a *Christian* soldier. Many soldiers are doing that by going on foreign soil where it is illegal to mention the Gospel. As a Christian, we are bringing God's kingdom with us everywhere that we go. What an awesome opportunity to be able to do that *with* pay and benefits! In the military community we would call this *being deployed.*

But even if a Christian soldier is not deployed overseas or if he spends his entire military career on local soil, his job is still to be Christian. Remember, we are all missionaries. We wives must continue to encourage our husbands to comprehend the impact they are making in God's kingdom. It's so easy for the soldier to become discouraged and to lose focus of his ultimate goal.

When a soldier is deployed overseas, he accomplishes

many tasks that he might not mention to you (or the ones the media does not emphasize). Some of the work that soldiers do while in combat zones includes protecting our country by keeping terrorism off our soil, freeing the oppressed from terrorist leaders, helping the local people obtain basic utilities and education, and assisting the nationals to build their own government and military so that they can survive on their own and protect themselves. This is only some of what soldiers do and the impact they make when deployed. And this does not include the other things they do as Christian soldiers.

Tips from Chapter 2

• Make an effort to talk to your husband today (if he is not deployed), and ask him what he does specifically. Ask questions. Encourage him in what he tells you, and let him know how important he is to you.

• Write Bible verses or encouraging quotes for him that relate to the military work that he does, whether or not he is overseas.

• Read *The Five Love Languages* by Gary Chapman and find out what your husband's love language is. *Speak* to him in his language.

• Take TRAITMARKER's *Finding Your Hidden Strength* at www.traitMarker.com (and request a token for your husband-soldier). This personality assessment is a great tool to understand how the small things about our personality make such a huge difference in the way we feel, think, and in the things we do.

• Constantly reinforce in your children the importance of what their father does, and build him up to be the hero that he is.

Questions from Chapter 2

• What are some ways you could personally encourage your spouse? Do you feel like you could improve in this area?

• What are some creative ways your children could help your husband feel especially loved?

• Do you set aside the time to spend with *just* your family to build each other up as a family unit? What are some activities you could share together to encourage this?

POINTS YOU WANT TO REMEMBER

feel free to jot down notes below...

Nicole Brocx Lee

POINTS YOU WANT TO REMEMBER

feel free to jot down notes below...

- CHAPTER 3 -

Aliens in a Foreign Land

The stranger who dwells among you shall be to you as one born among you, and you shall love him as yourself; for you were strangers in the land of Egypt: I am the Lord your God.

Leviticus 19:34

One question that always stumps me and leaves me completely dumbfounded is *What is your hometown?* When someone asks me that question, I usually stand there with a confused stare and then blast back questions such such as *Do you mean where was I born? Are you asking where I lived last? Do you want to know where I've lived the longest?* The conversation usually consists of me rambling on about various places I've lived and ending up with me talking about how much I love San Diego. My response is all over the place and leaves anyone within earshot confused.

My sons have had to fill out paperwork with the same question, and I have been no help in figuring out an answer for them. I *still* don't know the answer. Not only have I moved several times due to the military, but my family had also moved many times because we were an immigrant family. It doesn't help that I was born in Holland, that I'm a California resident, that I have a Tennessee driver's license, and that I live in Texas!

My Family's Journey

I was born in the Netherlands (Holland) from parents who were born in Indonesia. When I was a baby, we moved from the Netherlands to Nevada. My parents had a strong Dutch accent, and I often felt that I didn't fit in. Friends would say they couldn't understand what my parents were saying, and they would ask me over and over what country we were from. I had a little Mexican friend in kindergarten, Leticia. Because the other kids could understand that her parents spoke Spanish, I soon began telling my classmates that I was Mexican, also. Trying to explain the whole Dutch-Indonesian heritage was too difficult, and I was needlessly embarrassed. My classmates could grasp the fact that I was Mexican although I wasn't, so it was something I easily lied about.

Now, I am quite proud of my heritage. With the advances in correspondence due to the Internet, I am able to contact relatives (most of whom I have never met) and get to know them. In fact several of my relatives have actually found me on Facebook, including my half-sister and half-brothers, and it's been a delight to be in contact with them.

My father was a very intelligent man, although he had very little education. His education was halted when he was put into a concentration camp as a teenager. Although he only got the equivalent of probably a seventh-grade education, my father spoke about five different languages and loved to be with people of different cultures. He grew up in Indonesia, which at the time was called the Netherlands East Indies because it was Dutch-occupied territory in the city Batavia which is now Jakarta.

During WWII my dad, who was a teenager at the time, and his family were put into a concentration camp by the Japanese. While they were in the camp, my dad and his childhood friend were roomed with an older man. They took care of this man, getting him the food that he needed, etc. My father never knew what happened to the man in the concentration camp until a chance encounter on the opposite side of the world several years later.

My family moved to Washington when I was a teenager. My dad, who was a realtor at the time, came home from work one evening with a story for us. A man had walked into his office to buy a house, looked at my dad, and then started crying. My dad wondered why this man was staring at him in confusion and why he was so emotional. The man went on to share a story with my father that is completely remarkable even to think about now. Apparently, he was the son of the older man who my father and his friend had helped out in the concentration camp. This man's father had told his son the story of what happened at the concentration camp, sharing the last name of my dad. So when the man walked into my dad's office in Washington State and read the name-tag on my dad's suit *(Brocx* is a rare last name in any country), he couldn't believe his eyes.

The amazing ways that God can bring hope and encouragement after so many years and across so many miles is extraordinary. I am still always amazed at the *coincidences* that occur within my life and the lives of others. It's just proof that God is much more all-knowing than we can imagine.

Both of my parents were deported from Indonesia to the Netherlands in the 1950's where they met, were married, and had my brother, Andrew, and me. During that time, everyone who lived in Indonesia who was of Dutch heritage was forced out of the country by the Indonesians and sent back to Holland. Even though their families had lived in Indonesia for centuries, the Indonesian people wanted to claim their country back for themselves. Many died on the journey from Indonesia to Holland because of the extensive travel and extreme temperature differences. These former Indonesians had to go from living on tropical islands on the equator to the cold and wet climate of the Netherlands. This was difficult on so many levels. For many years after moving to America from Holland, my uncle (my father's brother) did not want to even visit Holland due to the prejudice he felt when he lived in Holland. The tall and fair-skinned Dutch people often didn't treat these short, dark-skinned *invaders* kindly.

My mom was also from Indonesia, although she never had to be in the concentration camps. She also moved with her family to Holland during the evacuation of the Dutch. My mom and dad met in Holland where my brother and I were born. From Holland my family moved to Nevada and then to California in search of employment. My father finally got a stable job as a welder in a company that employed a large number of Mexican immigrants. When we were at the dinner table, my dad would share these jokes that he learned from his Hispanic friends. He would laugh so hard he often had a difficult time even finishing what he was saying. My brother, Andrew, would laugh along with him, and I would feel completely left out because I had no idea what they were laughing about (and I felt a bit stupid because I did not understand these jokes). It wasn't until very recently, when speaking to Andrew, that he told me he had no idea what my dad was saying but was only laughing because he found that my dad laughing was so hysterically amusing! In reality my father was taking a joke that was said to him in broken English (Spanglish), translating it in his mind from English to Dutch, and then relaying it to his family. No wonder I had no idea what he was talking about!

Different Things to Different People

In addition to differing languages, every culture has different sayings that make sense *only* to that ethnicity. One of the sayings that my family used to say was *an ant on a curtain.* It was said in Dutch, but I knew the meaning. I thought they were saying *an aunt on a curtain,* and I always wondered why my aunt would be clinging to a curtain and what that had to do with anything that was being said. It was a saying that is similar to *a fly on the wall,* meaning that one is able to freely observe without being noticed: not that one's aunt is hanging from a curtain in a house!

As there are many sayings that don't cross the cultures of other nations, there are also many sayings that are used in one part of the country and not in another. Being in the military and moving from one side of the United States to the other, I was able to experience this first-hand. While in the military, my family moved from the West Coast to the Deep South. Talk about a culture shock!

We drove across the country from Washington State to North Carolina. We initially could not understand a lot of what the local people were saying. Not only was the southern drawl thick, but the sayings were completely different than any we had ever heard. I remember the first time someone said to me *Give me a holler when you're done.* He was one of our pastors, and I was in the sanctuary working on a teen girls' retreat. I looked him in the eye and asked "So you just want me to yell when I'm finished?" He laughed and explained to me that it was a saying that merely meant to let him know when I was finished and not literally yell for him. Thankfully, I cleared that up before he left. After living in the South for over 15 years, I don't give it a second thought when someone tells me they are *fixin* to do this or that, or when someone refers to one person as *y'all*. In fact, sometimes I catch myself saying things with a bit of a southern accent. Ok, I don't catch these idiosyncrasies myself but others who I haven't seen for a while (or who are not from the South) will notice at times.

Feeling Like a Foreigner

As with someone born in another country and having to move far away, living the life of a military wife has the potential of making one feel like a foreigner. Because we are often sent to places that are not of our own choosing and are completely foreign to us, it is like we are a displaced people. My family had the privilege of living in the same place for much longer than most military families (although it's the least favorite place I've ever lived) which has provided our sons with deeper roots than many military families. We did live thousands of miles from our nearest relatives at the time, and that part was difficult. But when you feel like you've got a bum deal, think of people who have struggled more than you have – it puts your life in perspective.

As a military wife, realize that the location to where you are sent is *your* territory, just as much as if your spouse is sent to a foreign land. Believe me, it usually seems as if you are sent to the location where you would least choose to live. We lived in our last location, Tennessee, for over 10 years. It never felt like home to me, and it often seemed like I was in a desert, not literally but figuratively. I know that much of this was because Mike was gone much of the time, but it also just seemed like a struggle to find myself feeling at home. Before Tennessee, the longest I have ever lived anywhere in my life was four years, and I didn't even grow up in a military family. I constantly had to refocus and shift my mind from the victim mentality that we are prone to fall into. I had to remember that although I don't necessarily get to choose were I live, God is in control and had placed us exactly where He wanted me and my family to live. I believe that God had placed me and our entire family in a situation to really allow me to learn to trust Him and not completely to rely on circumstances around me.

I have several friends who were born and raised in other countries, married military men when their husbands were stationed in their homeland, and then made the transfer to jump across the world to our foreign land of the United States. I have made friends with military spouses who are from countries that include India, England, Bolivia, Russian, Chile, Argentina, Korea, the Philippines, and Mexico.

One of my dearest friends is an undocumented illegal. No, she's not here to try to take our jobs or involved in the drug trade. She is, in fact, the wife of a soldier who is frequently deployed and fighting for the freedom of the United States. You may ask *Why didn't she just stay in her own country and make the best of what she had?* Well, why didn't our ancestors just stay in their own countries and make the best of what they had? Our country is merely a couple of hundred years old, and unless you are a 100% Native American it wasn't until recently that your family uprooted itself to come to this new land.

There are a multitude of reasons people immigrate to the United States: job opportunities, family, fleeing oppression. I am aware that there is the legal and correct way to come into the country which is always the best route if possible. I know that for my family there was a five-year waiting period to come into the country (once we found a sponsor). So we had to wait until my aunt and uncle had lived here for five years before following them. But we were not fleeing from oppression or opposition. My family was just moving to begin a new life in a new country. There are many verses in the Bible that come to mind when I hear people complaining about *those people* coming into the country to steal their jobs, etc. In the Old Testament there is verse upon verse about welcoming the alien in the land, and also about treating them as equals. Leviticus 19:34 says *The alien living with you must be treated as one of your native-born. Love him as yourself, for you were aliens in Egypt. I am the Lord your God.*

Evita's Story

There are several reasons that my friend, Evita, came into the United States illegally. Oppression is one of the reasons. Evita was a new mother with a young son, Amadis. Her son's father was in jail and soon to be released. This man would frequently beat up my friend, often knocking Evita unconscious. She was definitely afraid of his release from jail. As in his country, unlike the United States, no laws protect the abused woman. During the time Amadis's father was in jail, she met and fell in love with a military man, John, who had come across the border for recreation. Their plan was to get married, then move Evita and Amadis back to America with him. In the course of going through the marriage, it was found out that John was still unknowingly married to a woman who he thought he had been divorced from for several years. It was a quick marriage that John believed had ended within a few months. Apparently, the ex-wife did not go through with the divorce paperwork as he had thought.

Because John had to be back in the States to go through his schooling (he had gotten out of the military to try a civilian occupation but eventually went back into the military because the pay and benefits were a more secure way to make a living for his expanding family) and Evita had to flee the country with her son to prevent further injuries to herself (her baby's father told her that he would kill her once he was released from jail), they decided to go ahead and come to America. They would deal with Evita and Amadis becoming citizens once they got into the country.

Things did not go as planned *by any means*. I hear so many people tell me "These illegals just need to go through the paperwork to get their citizenship. It's not that difficult." It has been an expensive and lengthy process for Evita, John, and their family, and they are only now inching towards their goal of citizenship. Evita has been trying to go the legal route through the government to get the paperwork for herself and her son for over 9 years now. They have poured almost $9,000 into the process. They have tried to use lawyers who have given them false information which has caused them to do needless paperwork at an immense cost with little benefit.

After all of these years, they are just beginning to see progress (they finally found a lawyer via a friend who is going after citizenship for his family, also). It's a shame that this could not have happened sooner. I have not heard the latest of what is to come of their legalization, but I think it hasn't progressed any further since I first wrote this chapter a few years ago.

John and Evita have legally married several years ago and have 3 more children together. John has been in the military a total of over 17 years and has been on several deployments to other countries. During one of the times when John was overseas, Evita received a letter in the mail from the immigration service saying that she and Amadis could be deported and would not be allowed back into the United States for 20 years. She went to a lawyer in town (prior to finding the one that she is using now) who told her it was a lost cause and she should sign custody of her children over to her husband.

Evita went to her husband's work where they had no choice but to bring him home early from his deployment. This created problems for him in his work, causing him to be reassigned, losing special pay, and not being able to be deployed or promoted for a while. Due to John's lowered income, they were not able to complete the immigration papers within the three-month period that was allotted them, causing them to start the *entire* process over from the beginning. At that point it was as if the total $9,000 had gone down the drain.

There is so much that Evita and Amadis cannot do because they are not legal citizens. They cannot work due to not being able to get a social security card. They cannot get a driver's license, which is a huge burden for a woman whose husband is often deployed. Both she and her son cannot further their education, and, of course, scholarship opportunities are completely not available. Evita and her son have been active in the local church for many years, pouring into the lives of others with their time and energy. Evita has helped in the children's ministry, teen ministry, women's ministry, small groups, and also with the military wives' ministry. Amadis has always followed after his mother's example in being a servant to all in need and stepping up to be the man of the house when John is not home. Evita and her family are thankful for all that the church has done to help in their situation: pray, provide character reference letters for her while doing her paperwork, and finding the lawyer they are using now (her pastor helped to find him). But what could the church have done more to help?

When I presented this question to Evita, she replied that if the church (all members) could have come together and been a better source of helping her find information and using the resources that others know about, then it would have saved her family much heartache and financial pains.

I also personally believe that the church should help those in their congregation with financial needs. Where your treasure is, there your heart will be also, Luke 12:34. I know that there are many churches that do, and helping the immigrant is definitely a way that speaks the love of Christ to those in need.

Needs of Immigrants

We are now living in a city that borders Mexico and has over 80% Mexicans in its population. There are many locals here who don't speak English. My husband's mother is Mexican and speaks fluent Spanish, and I always wondered why in his generation most don't speak Spanish even though their parents do. The same is true of my family. I can understand Dutch a bit when I hear it, but I was not taught the language. I was in the post office last week when I overheard the teller talking to the man ahead of me, and what he said really made sense to me. When he was growing up in El Paso, there was a strong separation between the Mexicans and the White people, and it was very apparent in the schools. He remembers that when kids would speak Spanish or if they opened their lunch boxes and there was a burrito in it, the White kids would beat them up. So, in order for them to blend in, they really needed to deny their culture and adapt to the White people's ways.

That is why so many Mexican parents and immigrants from other countries really tried to ensure that their children would not be set apart socially from the other kids: so they made them speak only English. Unfortunately, this has caused their native language to be lost in one generation. The postman said that now there is a shift here in El Paso: if you look Mexican and don't speak Spanish, then people look down on you. There are many areas in El Paso where the language spoken is predominantly Spanish only.

Needs of Military Families

For military of the families that get stationed overseas, the transition into another culture can be difficult and entail many of the same struggles that those of immigrants. My best friend, Deana, has been married for 25 years, and her husband is retired Air Force. Her family moved to Germany after living in North Carolina where we met them. He worked at aerial ports, loading aircraft and passengers, handling hazardous materials and logistics that needed to take place to run an airport while in Germany. Here is what she has to say:

Germany was scary immediately following 9/11. You didn't know who you could trust or where you could safely go. Everyone looked like they could have been a terrorist. The base pounded into our brains to always check our cars for bombs or other explosives. So I was trained on what to look for which was good but extremely intimidating, especially since I had little kids with me (my three sons, who were young then) all the time. We lived on the Air Force base in Frankfurt, Germany and right along the flight line for the international airport. There were several nights when we would wake up to the sounds of aircraft that we thought were headed right into our bedroom. The thought of another terrorist attack was always on our minds. As Americans, we were huge targets. But there was nothing for the families to help us deal with all this: nothing. We had each other, and since we are Christians we had hope in Jesus. But those that didn't have Jesus drank a lot, got in trouble, and just numbed their pain the best they could.

My own husband had to deal with issues even though he never went to Iraq. He had to hose down the insides of planes that were carrying shot up vehicles that were covered in blood from being attacked. From just looking at all the blood and blown up vehicles, my husband knew that most of those crews never had a chance. He also had to transport the bodies--and there were a lot of them--mostly young soldiers in the coffins headed back to be buried by their families. Still the chapel offered nothing: no support, no friendships, not anything. In fact our chaplain seemed to be only concerned with his rank, and he let everyone know about it too

Unfortunately, Deana's experiences with the chapels and the chaplains that her family came into contact with were not the most positive:

The chaplains would deploy with the troops and leave someone in charge that had no idea of what to do with the needs of the community. I tried to teach Sunday school to the Jr. High kids and was rejected because I was a Christian! The chapel's system is a joke for the most part. When a friend of mine thought her husband had been shot down in Iraq, she called me to come over because she didn't want to have face the chaplain alone, since he was no comfort to her at all.

As with any experience, there are the positive and negative aspects. Many people have wonderful experiences living overseas, but there are always challenges to being in a foreign location and culture. Tristen has been married four years and her husband has been in the military for over 20 years. They have 5 children combined: one is her biological son (8), and she is also raising his three youngest (11, 14, and 16):

Three years ago we moved to Harrogate, England. We were very excited about our adventure, but reality set in very quickly. The smallest things were way more difficult there. I found out I couldn't cook there. Nothing turned out right even when we followed the directions. Something as simple as slice and bake cookies were ruined frequently. Even my award-winning-biscuit-making Gramma couldn't make biscuits for us!

The weather was quite a shock for a Georgia girl like me. It rains every single day. We didn't even own an umbrella. It never gets above 72 F, and the daylight hours are way *different. In the winter the sun only shines from about 10:00 a.m. till around 4:00 p.m. Seasonal depression set in for us and for most of the American families we knew. It was also a struggle only being able to take one car as well as learning how to drive on the wrong side of the road. It was also very expensive, and moving into a house took every dime we had. It added up to over $10,000 for our move-in. It was also very hard knowing we couldn't drive to our families if something ever happened. You don't realize how hard it could be to get to your parents until you are actually there. Work obligations and money would have prevented us from coming home in emergency situations. My husband's job was very demanding.*

Despite all of the difficulties, Tristen takes everything is stride, and I really see her as a woman who takes advantage of every opportunity. Even with the challenges of a blended family and the fact that she has to move often being a military spouse, she has an upbeat view of life, and she really makes the most of every situation. Her last move was from Georgia to El Paso, Texas, and she has embraced the differences in climate, culture and location. She has mentioned several times how much she enjoys living here. She now lives on the opposite side of the United States from what is home to her, but she is making the most of life. Says Tristen:

I love military life. I love moving. It's always an adventure and I never get bored. (Keep a look out for the rest of Tristen's story in the chapter *Deployments Affect Marriages...*).

There is more to Tristen's story later. With both military and civilian families, it is always important to remember that no matter where we are living, our location is temporary in the scheme of things. While on this earth, we could move due to job relocation, family obligations, financial security, whether or not we are in the military. The important thing to keep in mind is that we need to make the most of the time that we have on earth. That includes the big things like relocating our families as well as all the monotony involved with getting accustomed to our new location.

Tips from Chapter 3

• Each person has a story, so take the time to find out about the people that are around you.

• If you meet someone of another culture, ask them questions about their childhood, how their country is different than America, how different the foods, holidays, and politics are.

• If you have moved to a location that is different than your home, visit places that are different than those to which you are accustomed. Try new food, and enjoy the differences in the culture and activities.

Questions from Chapter 3

• Are you close to many people of differing cultures and backgrounds, or do you tend to stick with whom or what you're most comfortable? What are ways that you could get to know other people with ethnicities different than your own?

• Do you frown and gag at different foods when you are traveling or when you move, or do you try the local cuisine with an open mind? Do you encourage your children to try different foods and learn about different cultures?

• What does the Bible say about us accepting and loving others unconditionally, and what can you and your family do to improve and build on this?

POINTS YOU WANT TO REMEMBER
feel free to jot down notes below...

POINTS YOU WANT TO REMEMBER
feel free to jot down notes below...

- C H A P T E R 4 -

Inevitably the Inevitable Will Occur

*Be sober, be vigilant; because your adversary the devil walks around like
a roaring lion, seeking whom he may devour. Resist him, steadfast in
faith, knowing that the same sufferings are experienced by your
brotherhood in the world.*

1Peter 5:8-9

There is a big difference between being paralyzed by fear
and being prepared for what might occur. I'm not sure if we
wives simply perceive situations to be more severe when our
husbands are gone or if it just appears that way because we
are the only hands-on parent at the time. Either way, it really
shouldn't come as a surprise when things happen, because as
The enemy (the devil) comes to steal, kill and destroy. Fear is
one manifestation of that enemy. It knows that we are
separated from our other half and wants to turn our lives into
a turmoil and frenzy. It wants to steal joy. If we are prepared
in every way possible, then we are more easily able to stand
in the storms that life throws us without being shaken and
destroyed when these disasters or events occur.

Of course, there are so many things that one just can't
anticipate. After so many deployments and so many near
disasters, I have learned to roll with the punches. Of course
that's easier for me to say now that my husband's
deployments (since we have moved to El Paso) are to
locations like San Diego and Tuscon instead of Iraq and
Afghanistan. I will share some of my greatest memories of
how I coped. This will give you a glimpse of the many things
that military women encounter and the grace and ease with
which we can handle these situations. Ultimately, I am

sharing these stories so that you can see that I am human and that maybe you could learn from the many things I have done wrong.

Kitchen Mayhem

I once had a grease fire in the kitchen. I turned the stove onto HIGH to heat oil, then I made a quick trip to the bathroom, not thinking about the oil on the stove. This was not the brightest move on two accounts: why did I turn the stove to HIGH with grease, and why did I think I could make a trip to the bathroom with boiling grease on the stove? When I came back to the kitchen, I saw fire rising higher and higher from the stovetop. My sons were in the living room with a friend of theirs, watching television and completely oblivious to the smoke swirling around them.

The first thought that came to my mind was *Never use water to put out a grease fire.* I also remembered something about baking soda, or was it baking powder? It didn't matter, because both of those ingredients were near the flames. So in a mad frenzy, I grabbed a pitcher that was sitting in the kitchen sink, filled it with *water,* took a deep step back, and threw it on the mounting flames. Lo, and behold, it put the fire out! I don't think it was so much the water I used, but the force with which I hurled it.

My sons were in the living room doing their home-schooling since it was the middle of the day (actually, they were really watching television with their friend, Man, who frequently resided in our home). Smoke immediately filled the house, and I rushed the boys outside with a lot of yelling and screaming on my part. I didn't call the fire department, because it just didn't seem necessary to me because I had already put the fire out. And, of course, I waited to call our insurance company (because it's one of my greatest delights, being on the phone for hours with various companies and spending countless minutes listening to elevator music and dealing with getting details situated before finally speaking to a human... not!).

It was several days later when I called the insurance company. After they made me feel like a complete child, due to the untimely manner in which I called them, the fact that I didn't call the fire department, and didn't have a fire hydrant in my house, they got the information they needed and sent people to clean up the damage.

The people who were sent to assess and clean up the results of the fire were wonderful. They helped me itemize all of our charred and smoked possessions, even adding things that I didn't even know I could itemize. I actually got a new paint job out of it, a new microwave, and a little over $1,000 for the damaged items (many of which were just junk to me). Yes, it was a complete pain, because we had to leave our house for several days while they did the repairs. The day the painters came, my oldest son, Keir, was just coming back from a two-month-long mission trip. He was completely exhausted, and we had to eat all of our meals out. Thankfully a friend let us stay at his house while the painters and cleaners worked on our house and while he was at work, and we were able to go to our own homes and sleep each night. The $1,000 was an added blessing that would have been great to use for debt, (but most likely we used it for other things).

As with anything, we should learn from every experience we encounter. What did I learn from the fire? One thing is to make sure to have adequate insurance to cover all of your possessions and insurance that is adequate for where you live. We had a horrible flooding in our city that hadn't been that bad since the Civil War. Consequently, most people did not have flood insurance (which was separate from regular homeowners insurance). It was quite devastating to our city, and much of the damage is still being fixed now almost 3 years later. So when moving to a new location, make sure to check into whatever special insurances your area will need: hurricane, flood, hail damage, etc. If you live in an apartment, it's important that you have renter's insurance to cover the cost of your possessions in case of theft or damage.

Medical Issues

We've also had many medical emergencies while my husband was deployed. During one of my husband's first deployments to Iraq my two youngest sons, Rainier and Theo, both had the chicken pox. They acquired them two days after my husband left for his deployment. Keir, who was the only other driver in the family at the time, was on a mission trip, as it was summer (every summer from the time he was 12 years old until after he graduated from high school, he was involved in a mission's trip to various countries). While I supported this and loved the opportunity for him to go, it almost always was while my husband was deployed so that both of the men of the house were gone at the same time, year after year.

As my remaining sons were young at the time, I couldn't even go to the store to get groceries. The boys had extremely severe cases of the chicken pox. Not only were they miserable, but they were highly contagious. I think people did not realize that I needed help with the most basic of needs. I finally had a good friend, Asdrubal, who was the pastor of a Hispanic church, call me and ask if I needed anything. I asked if he would please go to the store at midnight to buy popsicles for the boys who couldn't seem to keep any liquid down. I am so thankful for those who helped in ways that may have seemed insignificant. Sometimes it's the little and most simple of things that make the biggest impact.

My second-born son, Dane (who was 12 at the time), broke his arm twice during one deployment. The timing of the first break was inconvenient. My oldest, Keir, (then 16) was leaving for a mission trip for the summer (this was a different year than the fire incident). About a week before he left on the trip, the boys were playing on the trampoline and Keir landed on Dane's arm. Dane had a baseball game that day, and although Sherry, my long-time friend who was visiting, kept telling me that Dane's arm was broken, I brought him to the baseball game because he was pitching that year! I was sure there was no way his arm could be broken. Obviously, he didn't get to pitch, and everyone at the field told me that it was definitely broken.

At the emergency room after hours of waiting to be seen and then waiting for the x-ray results, it was confirmed that his arm was broken. They casted it. Not only was he out of baseball for the entire season, but he had to miss going to *Six Flags* for the long-awaited homeschool trip we were all planning to go on the following day. Thankfully, we had friends who took Keir and my third-born son, Rainier, and I stayed home with Dane and Theo (the youngest who was only about 5). Just a few days later, Keir left for his summer-long mission trip, leaving me with the 3 younger sons, the eldest now with his newly-broken arm. Later that year, Dane would once again go to the emergency room with a break, this time his shoulder. Again the break occurred with the assistance of Keir (this incident was during an indoor board or card game, believe it or not). Yes, boys can be rough! Dane's shoulder was not casted, but he was supposed to wear a shoulder sling that looked like a funky backpack. He chose not wear it in public, and thankfully his shoulder healed with no complications. Dane has not broken a bone since that year.

Other physical ailments often would happen when Mike deployed. Horrible as it sounds, I am thankful that these occurred in my sons and not in me, as I am the caregiver. Rainier had a ruptured appendix a week before his 16th birthday. He had been complaining of stomach problems for quite awhile. The stomach virus was going around at that time, and his symptoms seemed to be the same. They were identical, but his just seemed more pronounced. I put off taking him to the hospital because I figured he would just be better getting the rest he needed at home. After Mike left for another of his deployments, Rainier's symptoms were so intense that he actually begged me to take him to the emergency room. I sure felt like the incompetent parent. The nurses assessed him and said that his appendix was enlarged but not ruptured, so they performed several other operations before his due to a higher number of car accidents than normally occurred. When they were finally able to operate on him, they found out that indeed his appendix had ruptured. What had begun as an operation that would have us leaving in a few hours turned into almost a week-long stay at the hospital. I am so thankful that my oldest sons were still living at home to take care of Theo and our dog. I stayed in the hospital with Rainier the entire time, just going home during the day to shower when I was able to get away. My sons who were home would bring me food, and I also had a good friend bring my boys some meals. It was an exhausting experience. When we were finally able to come home, I think we slept like babies for a few days straight.

One of the biggest things that I have learned in most of the various things that have happened that beyond our control is not to assume that others know how to help you. Other people do not know what your needs are, and if they have never been in the situation that you are in, they most likely don't even know that you need help. If you have some good friends who you know that you can count on, let them know what your needs are before you feel like your situation is at a catastrophic level. Most people are more than willing to help, but they won't *automatically* know what your needs are.

Trouble with Cars

I have also had two car accidents while my husband was deployed. One was while traveling from Tennessee to North Carolina to visit friends. Just beyond the halfway point into the trip about five hours into the drive, we hit stop-and-go traffic due to road construction. I decided that it would be an opportune time to take my eyes off the road to change the music. The van was rolling along slowly but not slowly enough before I realized that the car ahead of me was at a dead stop. Thankfully, no one was injured. It was completely my fault, but the man whose car I hit was very kind and didn't berate me for being so reckless.

Prior to traveling before Mike left for overseas, Mike and I had just visited some wonderful, lifelong friends, Bob and Jeanette, who told me "If you ever need anything while Mike is gone, please call us and let us know". As soon as I got in the accident, I could hear Jeanette's words ringing melodiously in my ears. I pulled off the freeway and into a parking lot, called Jeanette in a panicky sob, explaining that I had gotten into an accident. When Jeanette asked me where I was, all that squeaked from my throat was "In front of K-mart." I had no idea what city I was in. When I finally calmed down, I walked into the store and figured it all out. There was a car shop nearby, and the extremely nice gentleman temporarily fixed my smashed radiator. There was so much damage for what seemed like such a light impact. When we finally arrived in Fayetteville, my four sons and I intact, I took the van into the shop to be fixed. I had to wait over two weeks for the part to be sent and the van to be completed. That extended our visit with my dear friends, so I definitely wasn't complaining.

The other car accident I was involved in was much more traumatic. Several years later while on the freeway heading to a baby shower, I was driving in the right-hand lane when suddenly I felt and heard a BOOM! I could tell that my car was being pushed and then began spinning around in circles on the freeway. All I could remember to do was pray out loud that another vehicle would not hit me and that I wouldn't get hurt. When I finally came to a stop, I tentatively got out of the car and looked around. I was in the median of the freeway within inches of the traffic, going in the opposite direction from where I was headed! A few men had gotten out of their cars and were walking towards me, asking if I was okay. My reply was a very weak, "I'm not sure. I think so, but am I bleeding?" I'm so blessed that absolutely nothing was wrong with me physically. As for the car, we had just bought it at a great bargain from a friend immediately before Mike deployed. Sadly, it was totaled. A college student traveling home to surprise his mother happened to be driving a short distance behind me and could see the whole thing. Thankfully, he stopped to speak to the authorities because it was a hit-and-run and no one else saw what had happened.

Apparently, a huge semi-truck to my left sideswiped me and pushed me along the freeway for a short distance. The driver sped off after I was no longer in his way and took off. I spun in circles to the left and wound up spinning into the median. I was fortunate that my car stopped when it did because I was a few inches from the oncoming traffic which was slower than normal that day. Keir had just moved back home for one month before he moved across the country and wasn't working at the time. I called him crying, and he came to pick me up. Although this accident could have been horrific, I can really see the hand of God on the entire situation. I am very thankful that things did not go worse, that no one was hurt, and that the young man took the time to stop and help me out. Because the car was totaled and we got such a good deal from our friends on the purchase of it, we actually got *more* money from the settlement than we paid. I surely would have preferred not getting in an accident and keeping the great 40-mpg vehicle, but once again I am very, very thankful.

Additional Preparation Tips

I am not the only wife whose husband deploys and things seem to go awry. A friend shared some things with me recently. She is a young wife whose husband deploys often. She knows what it's like to have her husband gone for both good events like birthdays, anniversaries and holidays and well as for tragedies. Her grandmother just recently passed away during her husband's latest deployment. Because her husband is in a special operations unit, she often can't share information with people she knows. She says,

I don't even know that he'd be able to call me even when he finds out information. Not many know he's gone, and I can't say much about it.

Hearing her say these words really brings back so many memories of times when I was not able to be involved in major events with my husband. The fact that our men are deployed during such huge occasions in our lives really amplifies the loneliness of their absence in these special moments. It's difficult to explain to those around us who have not been in that situation, and there are times when we are not able to discuss it with anyone due to the missions our husbands are involved in when deployed.

One thing that is so important for a wife while the husband is deployed is to make sure she knows where all of the paperwork is so that it's easily accessible. Make sure the car has all of the current insurance paper, registration etc. Organization in all areas, especially paperwork, helps situations run more smoothly and with less hassle. I am definitely not a neat freak, and I often pile papers, but I cannot stress just how much easier your life can be and how much time you will save if you are able to organize your papers and belongings. Different people organize their belongings in different ways, so find out what works best for you.

There are many situations that seemed like such huge ordeals at the time and are such discouragements and distractions. It's easy to let these moments cause despair, and it is so important to know that we are not alone in these moments that can just take us captive. I know that a large percentage of women whose husbands are deployed are on some sort of anti-depression or mind-altering medication. I find this to be very sad. As military wives, we are often just in need of other people who are willing to help us out or even just listen to us. Looking back at the times I was without my husband due to his numerous deployments, I find it quite interesting that the people who helped me most were neither in the military nor from my church. I find that disturbing because the church is supposed to be our family, especially when we have no family nearby. But at the same time I am so thankful for the wonderful people that God has always placed in my life to be an encouragement and blessing to me and to my family.

During Mike's Last Deployment

Before Mike's last overseas deployment, I had a long list of goals that I had set for myself, because I figured that I would have plenty of time to accomplish them while he was gone. This was a nine-month deployment (which most of them were), and as I had only two sons left at home who were both in high school, I figured I would have a little more free time than usual. Apparently, God had other plans for our family than my completing my to-do list.

The very day that Rainier, Theo and I brought Mike onto the military post for him to head overseas, I received a call about one of the friends of my oldest son. This boy had gotten into some trouble with the law due to family squabbles. If no one would agree to take him into their home, he would be stuck in a juvenile detention facility. He was 17 and only had his senior year of high school to complete, so Mike and I figured it shouldn't be too much of a hassle to help him out. Mike's flight was delayed for a day, so I was able to discuss this all with him.

We couldn't have been *more wrong* in assuming that entire situation would be remotely uncomplicated. I not only had to take him to his court appointments which were over an hour-and-a-half away at least once a week, but his school was also the same distance away which meant that I had the long drive twice a week. I had spoken with his headmaster, Robbie Grayson, and he agreed that this young man could do most of his schoolwork at home. He only had to be brought to school once a week. These trips to his school increased as his level of irresponsible behavior increased. Our family was so thankful to Robbie for all of the love that he showed to this teen and for all the help that he provided for our family in this situation. It would have been close to impossible without his help. He has turned out to be a lifelong friend for our family and definitely a blessing all-around.

The constant commute was wearing on our car and my time, and the maturity level of this young man was way below what I had imagined. It was often like I was dealing with a much younger child in a teenage body. Getting him to do his schoolwork, dealing with his dishonesty and inconsistencies, and adjusting to the challenges of raising another child without the help of a spouse was a huge strain on our family.

When I first agreed to be his guardian, I was told that his church would contact mine so that I would have help. Sadly, that was not the case, and with only Robbie helping me from afar (mainly by phone and meetings in person as we were able), it was just too much of a responsibility for me to tackle by myself. We tried to set up rules and boundaries for both school and for the house so that he would improve his schoolwork and behavior. This caused the travel time to and from his school to increase, as we would have meetings with both Robbie and his mother to figure out the best plan of action for him.

We loved this boy dearly, and we always wanted what was best for him. Although there were many in our church who knew that we were in this situation, no one seemed to know what to do to help us or to even take notice that we needed help at all. At one point Robbie even called our church to request help for me and for the young man, but they just really didn't understand how to take care of us or were possibly not equipped to know how to handle our needs. And they never called him back after telling him that they would.

After six months of this teen living with our family, we came to the conclusion that it was in his best interest that he would move back to his own city so that his chances for actually graduating from high school would increase. He was not completing his schoolwork while he was living in our house, and it was really important for him to get his high school diploma. Somehow this idea of him moving back to his own city did not go over too well with the court system, and I was taken to court with the possibility of being fined and/or possibly jailed.

It's always frustrating being the *bad guy* for trying to help people. My husband wound up coming home from his deployment just a few days before the court date, so he was able to go to court with me. He didn't come home from his deployment early, but it was perfect timing that he was able to be there. The court situation turned out in my favor which was a huge relief! The lawyers and court people seemed to be doing their best to do what most beneficial for the child, although most times it appeared to be a circus act. It was surely eye-opening, and the teens and parents who were better at presenting themselves seemed to be given the benefit of their cases more often than not.

In the end, the young man was placed back in the custody of his family. He received his high school diploma with the diligent help of Robbie giving him many extra hours of schooling. Sadly, he is now estranged from his family. It really proves how one can only help a person so much, but that person must make choices for himself that determine the outcome of his life. Looking back, I'm not sure that we would have done anything differently as far as taking him into our home. I do believe that he was able to live in an environment where he was shown unconditional love for the six months that he lived with us, and it is our hope that he will one day look back on it all and realize that there is hope.

Things will happen when our husbands are gone that we just can't plan for in advance. That does not mean that we should be unprepared for what may occur. Remember that it is always best to be organized and situated in the areas that you do have control over so that when things happen that are not anticipated, they will not cause as much chaos as they potentially could.

Tips from Chapter 4

- Have a list of people who you can easily and quickly contact if you are in an emergency situation.

• If you know a military family, let them know if there is anything you can do to specifically help them. If you are able to fix cars, are able to fix appliances, or are willing to help with yard work or babysit, let the family know in advance what you can specifically do to help them. Follow through by reminding them. Often as a military spouse we don't want to bother someone who may have just said they would help to be nice. Let them know that you are really there to follow through.

• Make sure you know where all of your important papers are before your husband deploys. You don't want to be in an emergency situation and not able to contact him or have him get in contact with you in a timely manner.

Questions from Chapter 4

• What can you do to better prepare yourself and your family for emergencies that may occur? Do you have a backup plan or do you tend to just *wing it* in most situations? What can you do to improve on that?

• Do you know of other military families who have a spouse deployed or out training? What can you to do help them out? Even if you are limited on time, can you find some small things to do to help them that would be encouraging to them? What could your children do that would be a blessing to them?

• When you look back on previous incidents that have occurred in your family, can you find ways that you might have handled the situation differently? Do you feel like you are learning from things that have happened in your past? If not, how could you change that and learn from your past?

POINTS YOU WANT TO REMEMBER

feel free to jot down notes below...

- C H A P T E R 5 -

Unmentionables...

Do not be overcome by evil, but overcome evil with good.
Romans 12:21

What are *unmentionables?* The first definition I looked up for the word says *undergarments.* That's not the definition we want! The next definition says *not fit to be mentioned or discussed: unspeakable.* Another appropriate word is *taboo: something that is unacceptable to speak about.* In every circle and culture, there are things that are considered both appropriate and inappropriate. In the military circle, this list of unmentionables would differ significantly from the list that civilians would consider inappropriate.

I liken an *unmentionable* to an elephant in the room. This is the subject that or person who no one wants to talk about, but that/who everyone knows is there. Just because things are not discussed doesn't mean that they are not real. I looked up the term *elephant in the room* in *Wikipedia* to get a clear and accurate definition. An *elephant in the room* is an English idiom for *an obvious truth that is being ignored or that goes unaddressed.* The idiomatic expression also applies to *an obvious problem or risk no one wants to discuss. It is based on the idea that an elephant in a room would be impossible to overlook; thus, people in the room who pretend the elephant is not there have chosen to avoid dealing with the looming, big issue.*

Necessary Preparations

There are so many unmentionables and *elephants* unique to the life of a military family. One of the main discussions that military wives like to avoid is *funeral planning*. Most would think it to be morbid to mentally plan your own husband's funeral. As a wife of a man whose husband is in danger every time he deploys, it's not a frivolous thing to contemplate. I have attended several funerals of soldiers, and I have seen the pain that my husband shows when time and again he loses one or more friends who have become like a brothers to him. It has even entered my mind many times what songs I would play, what pictures I would show, and what I could do that would honor a life that could quickly be gone. I have spoken to other wives who consider these same things. In a way it is a comfort to us because although we cannot control what happens to our spouses while they are on deployment, we do know that the logistics of a funeral is something we *can* control.

In death we are reminded of the frailty and brevity of human life. It's never comfortable addressing these issues, but they are necessary. In all actuality, there are things that we as military families must do to prepare for a casualty. We definitely need to make sure that all of the paperwork is in order. When a spouse deploys, there is paperwork that needs to be completed and readily accessible.

The Power of Attorney (POA) papers are vital to have in order as we are the ones who will sign and act as our husband in his absence. There is a general POA and there are specific POA's. The specific ones cover various things like Federal Income Taxes and the purchase of large items like houses and cars, etc. Try to anticipate what you and your family will need before your husband leaves, so that you can be adequately prepared with the POA's. Also, be aware that businesses have the right to refuse your POA for any reason they choose. It may appear completely unfair to us as wives, and it's certainly inconvenient.

After going through many years of deployments and witnessing all the devastation that can and often occurs in many marriages, I can now understand how businesses and companies would be so strict to not simply allow the wife of a deployed soldier *all* the rights as the husband. One of the main reasons the companies are often strict is that it is fairly common for a wife to leave her husband while he is overseas.

One of the things these sorts of wives will do is secure their own financial stability. Some of the ways they can do this is by clearing out the bank accounts, racking up their credit cards (both for cash advances and for purchases), and leaving the house with everything cleaned out. It is common in the town where I lived to see many foreclosure signs in windows, and this was not because of the financial instability that is common in non-military parts of the country. This is due to the husband's being abandoned while deployed.

I have personally seen this happen when men return from deployments. They often have no idea that this is coming, and they are devastated. While I believe marriage to be a two-sided deal, I also believe that it *only* takes one side to make the decision not to make the marriage work. We have a good friend who is an Army chaplain. Several times when his soldiers returned home from their deployments, the chaplain would greet the returning soldier instead of the family. He would have the job of delivering divorce papers to the returning hero. It is quite sad and sobering.

It's not so unreasonable that a business would expect the spouse of a deployed soldier to have adequate paperwork and possibly to go through hoops, waiting longer than normal before approving a loan for a large purchase or withdrawing large sums of money. The companies are often doing this as a protection *for* the deployed soldier and also for their own business. This is especially true in cities with a large military population where they are more aware of these situations.

Some other situations that occurred during Mike's deployments involved paperwork. One involved the purchase of a vehicle. It is pertinent that both of your names are on the title and paperwork. Even if the finance people insist that it *is* in both of your names, *check* on the paperwork to make sure. Ours were only in his name, even when we told them to put it in both. This has happened with two of our vehicles, and it was inconvenient to get anything accomplished regarding them without Mike being present. Also, make sure accounts are in both names (electric, phone etc.) so that when he is gone you have access to them. The utility companies will not give you information or allow you to make changes simply because you are the wife: you must be on the account.

For example, I set up our cell phone account. But because I wrote his name *before* mine, they put it in his name. I didn't double-check and didn't know it was an issue until I tried to access information when he was deployed. I couldn't add a phone or even change our minutes. All I could do was pay the bill.

Counseling and PTSD

One huge unmentionable is counseling. I have run across so many people that have had many problems in this area. It seems like it would be something simple, but there are so many factors involved. Many times the soldiers go through such events that can cause PTSD (Post- traumatic Stress Disorder), and then there are all the factors that family members have that may cause them to be in need of counseling. The military does have services available to the soldiers and their spouses that cover not only physical needs but also mental. I am very grateful to have the military health benefits for those times when I have had to go to the emergency room. But what about those emotional traumas and catastrophes that can send our world reeling around us? Is the military the best place to go for the healing of our emotions and the handling of the battles that rage in our children? Much can and should be said about PTSD (Post-traumatic Stress Disorder).

This is such a relevant and common occurrence in many of the soldiers that go through deployments. The cases are so varied, and the different ways that people react also differ. It is often difficult to even know when someone struggles with PTSD. Many that battle PTSD don't like to admit it for many reasons. The first is because it would make them appear weak to the other guys with whom they work. No one wants to stand out as the guy who *couldn't handle it.* Another reason is that it may halt them in their career and possibly prevent them from going on other deployments or from completing their everyday jobs.

To those of us who have been in the military community for a while, it is often obvious that many are suffering from PTSD but that no one wants to admit that they have a disorder. That implies that something is wrong with them:

not that something happened that's beyond their control (which is often the case). Homicides, suicides, domestic violence, and breakdowns among military personnel are not so rare anymore. So many soldiers are worn out from frequent deployments that never seem to end and with no time in between to recuperate or process their prior-war experiences. There is much that can be done, and there are programs that are sprouting up to raise awareness and offer help. The church can and should be there to reach out to these hurting soldiers and their families in their congregation and communities. Most soldiers will not ask for help, but offering a listening ear, and having the resources available when someone does acknowledge the fact that something is not quite right would be a great first step for the healing of someone with PTSD.

Many different views exist about what PTSD really entails. One soldier, Brian, who has been on many deployments has his own take on the entire subject. I will leave it up to him to explain exactly what he feels about the matter in his own words (filled with a mixture of humor and candor).

Before I answer what I think about PTSD, I have to clarify the different levels of the military. First you have the guys on the ground who do all the fighting: we'll call them Grunts. Next, you have the people who support the Grunts. They provide everything from transportation to fixing our gear. We will call them Support Guys. Then you have the soldiers who do all the paperwork and all the behind-the-scenes stuff that keeps them far, far away from any real danger. We will call them by their acronym, POGUES, which stands for People Other than Grunts.

As far as the Grunts go, I firmly believe most of them have some sort of PTSD. But they handle it better because they were trained to operate in that environment and they are trained for the things they encounter. So the things they go through are not as much of a shock. Most Grunts are perfectly fine until someone comes along, usually a POGUE or Support Guy, who doesn't know his butt from a hole in the ground, and tries to get the Grunts to do stuff they know is stupid. We call this Disgruntled Government Employee Syndrome. I also believe that if a guy can prove he was a Grunt and can prove he was in combat, he should never be denied anything he needs and should be ushered to the front of every line he will ever find himself in from the Veterans Administration to Disney Land.

Support Guys are mostly guys who wanted to be Grunts but didn't have the drive to go be a Grunt. They like the show without having the go. They get to tell people they were in a high-speed unit and got to do some cool stuff, which they may get to do, but they usually take the story way too far to people outside the community and end up selling themselves as some great war hero. These guys from what I have seen will be the guys with all the unit stickers on their vehicles and usually try to claim some sort of PTSD when they decide to get out because they can't go any further in their job. And they try to rack up as many benefits as possible.

POGUES are probably the worst. I'm sure a lot of people have seen these guys at the PX. Usually they are a retired Sgt. Major who jumps out of his bling mobile with a handicap plate or hang-tag and it doesn't look like they miss a beat be-bopping into the PX or Commissary. These are the people we hate the most because these are the guys who end up writing books about the war that no one can relate to or remember the detail the guy writes about. They usually do one trip overseas where they starch their uniforms and get nice Army haircuts all while never leaving the base, but writing home with the best war stories. These are the guys who after spending their one deployment carrying an unloaded weapon come home and immediately claim PTSD so they can get the benefits and not deploy again. I could go on about POGUES, but let's just say I have not met one who genuinely could carry on a combat-related conversation without stumbling all over their own BS.

As far as PTSD in general goes, I compare it to the 1990's when every kid who didn't do well in school automatically was diagnosed with ADHD. In the Army if you heard a rocket hit a mile from your base: PTSD. If you stub your toe while dancing at Salsa night on the base: PTSD. Or if you get blown up and watch your friends die: the same

PTSD. It's hard to diagnose true PTSD because the symptoms are so broad and wide-ranging, but it doesn't take a genius to read between the lines and see that a large part of the PTSD crowd are full of crap.

PTSD *is* real. Brian is not saying that it isn't valid. He's saying that there are many soldiers who use the term falsely to get the benefits to which they feel they are entitled, valid or not. At the same time there are many who battle PTSD and struggle with it on their own and who do not get the help they need and deserve. There are extremes in both types of soldiers: those who need the help and those that abuse the help solely for the benefits.

Often PTSD doesn't show up in a soldier until years later with symptoms surfacing that hadn't earlier. More people are becoming aware of the issues of PTSD, and it is not taken as lightly as it had been previously. There is a great need for people to counsel effectively those with PTSD and not just put a bandage on the true issues with which soldiers deal. Often they will receive medication or therapies that bypass the real issues needed for permanent healing. The church should be able offer solutions on how to help those that are in need of healing and are in deep pain. Isaiah 61:1 says *The Spirit of the Lord God is upon me, because the Lord has anointed me to preach good tidings to the poor; he has sent me to heal the brokenhearted, to proclaim liberty to the captives, and the opening of the prison to those who are bound.* As Christians, this is what we should be doing: helping to heal those who are hurting and setting free those who are in bondage.

Someone with PTSD is definitely in need of healing and is in bondage. The church should have answers for the questions people are asking. We are not called to be perfect or to know everything. If we are not equipped help them, then we need to direct these people to where they can get the help that they need. I have seen too many people overlooked and shuffled around by people in the church, and it is understandable that those really seeking help would be disgruntled.

Needs of the Dependents

Children of deployed parents are also at risk of behavioral and emotional issues. There are so many hurting kids out there, and we really need to make an effort to keep our eyes and ears open to those children who would need help with their problems. I have a good friend, Shelby, who has had consistent behavior problems with her son, Jack. These difficulties stem from valid issues having to do with early childhood trauma and even a deep family tragedy that occurred right before he became a teenager (the death of his baby brother). Shelby has been trying to seek counsel for him in various ways. As her teenage son got older, he ran away several times, has been suicidal, and has even been hospitalized. Shelby has taken him to military counseling, Christian counseling, and has even asked two different churches she attended in different locations to help her family with their needs. This is Shelby's take on what has happened on her road through counseling:

It's hard to find a counselor who bases treatment on what God says – not just one who claims to be a Christian. Pastors we have had haven't had a clue! And our counselors have been flakes with very 'world-view' type advice. They would ask if Jack wants to hurt himself (which, of course, he would never admit). And if he did admit it, they would admit him somewhere and dope him up for 48-72 hours, then put him on maintenance meds and ask him the same questions again. How does that help him really deal with his problems? They are not even getting to the basic root of what the issues are.

I truly believe that good, Biblical counsel is something that every church should offer. I'm not suggesting that it is even plausible for every church to hire a certified counselor to have on staff, but it is possible to train people to be listeners and to educate themselves in the situations and lives of the people who are in their congregations. If a church has a high population of military people, the church needs to be relevant in helping them. Many people are just wanting a listening and compassionate ear that is backed with Biblical truths that would be sufficient to meet most people's needs.

Mike and I have counseled many couples and individuals, and it quite often just goes back to the Golden Rule: *Do unto others as you would have them do unto you.*

Budgeting

The last unmentionable is budgeting. I know this makes some people cringe, and sometimes I'm included in the category of those cringing. Finances are something that really needs to be addressed in every marriage. Whether or not you earn a small or large amount of money, it's important that you are diligent with the money that you have. As with all things, we need to be wise with everything that God gives us which includes our finances. Just as it is with time, if you spend it wisely and with purpose it will go a lot farther. It's easy for both time and money to be wasted if we are not really careful about budgeting them. One of the definitions of the word budget (Merriam-Webster dictionary) is *a plan for the coordination of resources and expenditures.* So when you budget, all you are doing is having a plan for how you are going to use your money.

The budget that a couple uses can be as simple or as complicated as the couple wants. There are some budget plans that allocate every dollar that is earned. We have tried this a few times but just never stuck with it because our needs shift constantly due to many factors: how many kids live in the house, how much my husband gets paid, special pays and deployments, medical expenses, travels, what gets broken, and the list goes on. For our family, we make a list at every pay period of what bills and expenses we have and work from there. We make an effort to put aside money for larger expenses that we have for the future, such as travels, holidays and birthdays, and we go from there. This works for our family, as the step-by-step budget is most often frustrating and more time-consuming than we willing to endure.

The important thing is that you find what works for your family, and make sure that you and your spouse are both are in agreement in all financial matters. Sadly, the number one cause of divorce in America is financial discord. This is not merely due to lack of finances but primarily not being in agreement with where and how the finances are spent.

In military families there are more things to address regarding finances and budgeting. For our family, I am the one who pays the bills and runs the budget. Mike is often not home long enough to pay the bills and allocate the funds based on deployments and travels, so it is more beneficial for our household that I be the financial planner. For many spouses this can be overwhelming if they are not used to being the ones who handle the finances. If the wife is equipped to do the budget before her husband deploys or leaves for an extended period of time, this would be less of a strain on their marriage and one less thing for either of them to worry about in the absence of one another. It is important to discuss finances with your spouse as early on in the marriage as you possibly can to avoid chaos and help the budgeting run more smoothly.

Jessica M. has been married for four years and has a young daughter. Her husband has been in the active military for about two years, and financial struggles are something that they definitely battled. Her family had moved less than a year ago from the Midwest to western Texas:

While in the Midwest, we were accustomed to a lifestyle with dual incomes and no children. That all changed once I had my daughter and mostly when we moved the first time. We had not adjusted our lifestyle (we had no budget before, so nothing to adjust!). We had just paid off our credit card debt with our recent tax return. Then we moved, we moved from a one-bedroom apt to a three-bedroom house. So we quickly furnished our house, thinking that we'd pay it off with the travel reimbursement. We did not think very hard, apparently, and thus found ourselves quickly falling back into debt.

With that came marital stress. My daughter also needed some new clothes, which I did not wisely spend. Having a girl is way too much fun! But thankfully, I realized what I was doing, stopped, and found some pretty awesome consignment shops and yard sale websites. I made a budget, but keeping to it turned out to be pretty hard. My husband needed Army gear which I quickly found out to be pretty expensive, and then his car did not pass inspection... so work needed to be done. We had depleted our savings account. We would make trips home, which is a 24-hour drive, even if we really couldn't afford it. I needed to make a trip to see my grandma whose health was failing, and we were unsure of how much longer she would live. Then I made another trip to see my brother in Georgia.

With the move to Texas, we were utterly unprepared for the financial toll that would take. Thanks to our neighbor's input, we thought we would get a lot more than we did. We asked for an advance on the pay to help with the finances for the trip. We bought a plane ticket for my father-in-law from Texas back to the Midwest, so he could help drive on the way to Texas. We paid for all his meals because he was unemployed. My brother and mother were with me, so we bought two hotel rooms each night we stayed over. We were allowed four travel days which we did in three days to help outset the costs. Once we got to Texas we quickly found a house that was about $70 more than our BAH (basic allowance for housing). We were planning on having another kid as soon as we arrived, so a three-bedroom house was what we wanted. Again, it was not what we could afford, but what we wanted. So, our debt continued to climb and was an argument my husband and I often had. He was a little more relaxed about it and I was not. There were a lot of nights where I had just wanted to give up, but I knew that wasn't an option. I told my husband I wanted to do marriage counseling or financial counseling, but he didn't think we had problems. We had gone from about $5,000 in credit card debt to $11,000 in just five months of living in Texas.

Jessica and her husband have had the chance to really discuss their finances and budgeting, and it has made a huge difference on the peace in their marriage.

After a few financial issues that Mike and I had due to his deployments, we figured out banking ways that worked for our family due to our unique financial needs. The first was that we asked our bank to put a hold on the debit purchases if there was not enough in the balance instead of allowing the transaction to go through and charging us a hefty fee. This also helped to prevent purchases from going through if there was no money in the account. It sure sounds like basic knowledge, but it has helped us tremendously as we were often not in the same location and couldn't contact the other about what the balance of the checking account. The second thing we did was open up a separate account for Mike that had money directly transferred into it for any spending needs he would have overseas. If he wanted to get me a gift or surprise me, he would be able to do it without it being on our joint bank statement. We keep this account open even if Mike is not deployed, instead of opening and closing it each time he is away from home.

As most families will make more money when the spouse is deployed, it's just as easy for that money to slip through our fingers if we are not diligent in keeping track of our finances. This is an area that I not only have seen in so many women whose husbands are deployed, but I have also witnessed in my own spending. I know that for myself I often eat out more when my husband is gone for several reasons. The first is that I am often too exhausted to cook. This was so true when I was raising my four sons and I was spending a lot of time taking them to and from their activities in addition to mine. It was always easier to pick up something to eat on the way home than it was to get home, cook a meal, and then eat.

Another reason that I believe women like to dine out while their husbands are gone is for the social aspect. It's always nice to sit down, relax, and chat with friends, especially when you have not had to prepare the meal. I think these are very valid reasons to enjoy a meal out, but if you are not wise in allotting a certain amount every pay period and planning that into the budget, you could easily find yourself in the middle of a pay period with no money to spare. I have done this more often than I'd like to admit, and I learned throughout the years to be wiser with my budgeting.

Another thing to consider adding to your budget when your husband is deployed are basic repairs and upkeep to the home and the car. While your husband is home, he is most likely able to do more of these things than you are able (or prone) to do by yourself. This is especially true if you have small children. If you have friends or neighbors who are able to help, that is wonderful. But sometimes it's just easier to hire someone and also more convenient for everyone involved. Make sure to add this to your budget instead of waiting until emergencies occur. Things will always break and upkeep will always be needed, so plan wisely and appropriately.

As with everything you do, if you plan in advance, something that could possibly turn into a tragedy will just seem like a momentary inconvenience. Try to do all that is possible to plan ahead so that situations and events that won't turn into something completely unbearable while your soldier is away or even at home.

Tips from Chapter 5

• Make sure that your car, medical, renters/mortgage insurance is all updated and all in one place before your husband deploys.

• It's wise to come up with a list of unmentionables before your husband deploys. Taking care of this list should be the priority before your husband leaves. For example, if you know that you need two new tires for the car, take care of it before his 6-12 month deployment. It's unlikely that those tires or an air conditioner on the fritz will last that long!

• If possible, schedule all medical and mental health appointments in for you and the family in advance. It's easier to accept that you might have a physical or mental health need if you routinely plan for check-ups.

Questions from Chapter 5

• What are the top five concerns that you fear facing in the absence of your spouse? Who would you turn to for help were your spouse gone? What plans or protocols do you have if they should occur?

• Does your spouse know your deepest concerns in his absence? If he doesn't, it would be a great opportunity and bonding experience for you both to talk about the unmentionables and to plan together for them.

• Do you have a budget? If you don't, what bothers you about coming up with a budget? If you draft up a generic budget, at least you will know what needs to be paid for (even if you don't follow it)... and knowing is half the battle.

POINTS YOU WANT TO REMEMBER

feel free to jot down notes below...

- C H A P T E R 6 -

Friendships

A friend loves at all times

Proverbs 17:17a

Friendships can either be very superficial or extremely deep. Many military wives frequently move and endure deployments while their husbands are gone. When it's understood that a location will be temporary, there is often a sense of urgency to relationships. This has the potential to cause unhealthy friendships. I have often jumped into friendships way too quickly and have learned that this was unwise. There is such a human need for sharing our lives and building relationships that sometimes caution is minimized. This is severely compounded by deployments. Our husbands are not with us, and we want to fill that role of companionship. It's wonderful and fantastic to have true friends that build us up and encourage us, but these types of solid relationships are usually built on time and trust.

True Friends

There are many verses about encouraging each other. One of my favorites is 1Thessalonians 5:11 which says *Therefore encourage one another and build each other up, just as in fact you are doing.* It is important that we find friends who encourage us in this way. There is a fine line between seeking out these companions who will build us up versus searching for people who say the right words to make us feel better. As my husband has deployed over 20 times, I know what it is like to sometimes be in a desperate search for someone to fill the gap of that companionship. Not everyone can be my *best* friend. We must carefully choose with whom we share our time and our heart.

I have a few people who I would consider true friends until the end. These kinds of friends are not common, and these relationships have been proven over time through difficult experiences. A military wife learns to treasure those friendships that run very deep. Often our closest friends are not based on proximity. We may initially meet due to a shared location, but the military sometimes moves us away from those we want to hang out with the most.

When my best friend, Deana, and I moved away from each other after spending almost every day together, we were devastated at first. It was so difficult to not have that one-on-one contact as often as we wanted to. We both had all sons, and we shared our daily activities with each other. We even traveled to other states together with all of our boys in tow. We had great adventures together. After being together fairly constantly for a few years, my family moved about 10 hours away so at least we were able to drive and see each other.

Six months after we moved, her family moved to Germany so that visits were not possible at all. This was before Facebook and Skype, so we became the postal service people's best friends with our frequent letters, cards, and packages. Now Deana and her family live about 10 hours away again. We are able to drive and visit each other, when family commitments don't take precedence, and we keep in contact via Facebook and frequent texting for the moment-to-moment activities. Technology has really improved over the years, and many can say that it has caused many to be less relational. For me, however, it's been a Godsend because I'm able to keep in contact with many more people with a less amount of time involved.

Putting Up Walls or Jumping Right In

Military wives often put up a wall in their relationships. It's easier to avoid getting close to someone, knowing a future move is eminent. Civilian wives may view military wives as being aloof when actually they are putting up a barrier to keep from being hurt.

That wall can easily come between healthy relationships for women. I have witnessed it, and I have been part of it. There are generally two unhealthy ways that we military wives embark on friendships. One is what I just mentioned: putting up a wall to prevent pain. The other is jumping headfirst and heart-long into a friendship. We realize that the friendship must be made in the short amount of time that we have with that person. What ends up happening is that person is often expected to meet our every need and fulfill all of our expectations—without the time that it takes to build trust. This tends to be intensified with husbands deployed. We expect that friend to meet our every need. It's just not realistic, nor is it healthy. I admit to falling into the latter category more than the former *wall-maker* category.

Unmet expectations lead to disappointment. Disappointment leads to bitterness. This is an unhealthy and vicious cycle. We recognize this cycle in unhealthy relationships between men and women that end badly. However, it is just as common in friendships. We do not need to set ourselves up for an unbalanced friendship. Expecting another person to meet all our needs leads to unnecessary hurt and pain that could be avoided. Indeed, there are friendships that begin quickly and become deep, but in most cases friendships take time and experience. Friendships are wonderful blessings and a great comfort. However, we need to be careful not to elevate those relationships to a level that is not beneficial to ourselves or the other person.

Healthy Friendships

Proverbs 12:26 says that *A righteous man is cautious in friendship, but the way of the wicked leads them astray.* This verse is confirmation that it is not wise to jump into any relationship. Those we hang out with will have an influence on us, either negatively or positively. We should not expect people to be perfect, but we need to surround ourselves with people who build us up spiritually and emotionally. One of my favorite Bible verses, and one that I always quote to my sons, the teens with whom I am in contact, or anyone that will listen is Proverbs 13:20 which says *He who walks with the wise grows wise, but a companion of fools suffers harm.* If we associate with people who are doing the wrong thing, we will be seen as one of them. It is not worth endangering our marriages and families to associate with others who compromise morals.

Not long ago I was in a situation where I *turned away* some friendships due to pains from other friendships I had jumped into without caution. I had hardened myself to be on the defensive (even paranoid), about how I perceived other women and their motives. At the time I saw it as being cautious, but now I can see how I hurt some women based on my own fears and prejudices. I have since asked for their forgiveness and restored these friendships. Unfortunately, our families have moved away from each other, and we are not able to spend time together—time we would have had if I had learned my lesson earlier. But God is so gracious at being a restorer, and I am very thankful for that. He is a God of second chances in so many ways.

We should spend the majority of our time with people who speak positively as opposed to negatively. It's easy for women to fall into the trap of being a complainer. The life of a military wife is extremely tough, and there is much that we can complain about. Complaining does nothing but cause us to be dissatisfied and discontent. When a person daily bombards everyone within listening distance about how the military is horrible, how her husband isn't meeting her every need, how her children are driving her crazy, etc., it's not long before her attitude of discontent rubs off on all of those surrounding her. It's not necessary to cut these people out of our lives, but we need people around us who can help change our outlook. Vanessa, wife of an Army man and the mother of four children, has this to say about church and friendships:

I have really thought many times about what I wanted or needed as a military wife. Things that I would love to tell young women that are coming into this environment like what to expect and how to be successful and honest with them. I want to tell them that it is hard but not impossible. So many precious young women come to church, and they just need to make new friends. And other women are older and they think they are better than the others because of their husband's rank when really we are all in the same boat.

The church, not just the leadership but also the mature members of the congregations, needs to reach out to new women and the younger women. This is something that I have seen lacking in many churches. Military families move so frequently, and they have to start new friendships and relationships every time they move.

Don't Limit Your Friendships

We should not limit our friendships based on age or our husband's profession. Our friends who are military certainly understand our differing needs based on having been through many of the same struggles. But sometimes others can get a view of us from the outside looking in that can be helpful in ways that another military spouse cannot see. I have a dear friend who has stuck with me for many of the years my husband has been on his constant rotation of deployments. She and her husband are not in the military, but she has been able to help me in ways that my military friends have not. Cheryl has been a listening ear to me even though she hasn't been through the experiences that I have. She has the compassionate heart that we are all called to have, not based on similar experiences but on her true love and compassion for others. She would listen with a caring and nonjudgmental ear and would have the courage to correct me if she thought I was complaining for the sake of complaining. She was always great at setting my eyes towards the real heart of the matter. We would sometimes go on weekend dates to a nearby city just so we could sew and do crafts in the hotel and unwind from our busy lives. She has a blended family with six children, so her struggles were different but just as intense as mine were. I do miss her dearly since we have moved, but I know that she will always be just a phone call or a text away if I need her.

It's important to not limit your friendships due to age. I have friends who are much younger than I am and friends who are much older. I think that my young friends give me a fresh outlook on life and are often not as hardened and skeptical as we can become when we get older. It's also nice to spend time with these younger women who are in a completely different season in their lives as their responsibilities are so much different than ours (maybe they are in college or have young babies). It's fun to be able to help them with problems that we have already gone through, and it's always great to be able to serve others. Another reason I love to hang out with those younger is because I enjoy doing several things that a lot of people my age don't enjoy doing. When we lived in Tennessee, we had an above ground pool. We would try to invite families over who were our age, but I often wound up in the house with the other wives. That was frankly quite frustrating to me! I learned that I needed to invite the college-aged girls swimming, because they would definitely love to accompany me in the pool.

I also find it vital to have friends who are older than me. I have been privileged to have several *mother* figures in my life who extended a helping hand and blessed me with their time and wisdom. I have two very dear mothers, Wendie and Jodie, who reached out to me when I was a young mother living in North Carolina. These older women taught many of us younger women to be exceptional housewives and to be compatible to our husbands. They were always there for us when we needed to talk, and they helped us when we had physical needs. Wendie's husband was retired military, so she understood the insides of the military life. Her children were also grown and out of the house, so she had the time to pour into so many of us. At the prompting of my good friend Jolene, who was a military wife and homeschooling four young children, Wendie started a class for us that we called *Keepers of the Home.* This class was based on Titus 2:4-5: *Then they (older women) can urge the younger women to love their husbands and children, to be self-controlled and pure, to be busy at home, to be kind, and to be subject to their husbands, so that no one will malign the word of God.*

We learned not only homemaking skills like cooking, entertaining, cleaning etc., but throughout these classes

Wendie shared her wisdom based on her experiences and her maturity. Through the years Wendie also taught quilting both in a quilting shop and at the home of a friend. Several ladies of all ages would gather once a week and not only learn the dying art of quilting but also soak in the stories of wisdom from a wide variety of older women. Wendie was always willing to provide us with these life-growing opportunities. In today's culture the practice of older women mentoring younger women is sadly lacking.

Jodie is another amazing woman who I call my *Mom*. It's wonderful how God places people in our lives so strategically. My husband and I led a small group through the church, and Jodie and her husband were placed in leadership over us. At first I was reluctant at the change in leadership, as the prior leaders were closer to our age and we were friends with them. I didn't feel like I would ever have anything in common with this woman who was older than me, nor did I think that she would be able to relate to me at all. I certainly was wrong. God knew exactly what He was doing, and He provided me with a caring *mother* who had many things in common with me and with whom I loved spending time. Even now after having moved away from North Carolina about 12 years ago, I still spend at least an entire day out of my schedule with Jodie when I visit, and I miss her dearly when I'm not able to see her often.

Friends for Life

Not all friends will be with you for your entire life. Some are there to carry you through a season or to be there for a certain period of time. Then there are the lifelong friends. Take time to foster these friendships. Friendships take time, energy, and unconditional love. We can learn so much from those who are different than us. We need to find the people in our lives who we treasure, and let them know how much we care about them and how much they mean to us. This is a great poem written by a friend, Mary Cleveland, for her close friends:

My sister my soldier my partner in crime
A mirror, an intrepid guide into the dark places in my heart,
You hold my hand and make me brave

To navigate the deep waters in the ocean of my soul
You expose your own heart to me
And help make me whole
During this season we're apart
Though together in heart
A little distance now But we'll be stronger somehow
After a journey, a trial or two
You will be amazed what God has done through and in you.
Though it seems we are traveling alone
We are with each other- anywhere we go is home.

There is one thing that I have noticed about my closest friends friends: I go to them for prayer and they keep me on the right track. I have seen this trait in my best friend, Deana, and in my new friend in the southwest, Barbara. This interesting characteristic is the fact that these dear friends are very much like my husband, and I am very much like their husbands! Both of these friendships are the rare kind that grew quickly and did not need much to flourish: God just placed these women in my life. Both Deana and Barbara are friends who I call on when I need prayer. I can count on them for that spiritual advice, and they know the same to be true of me. Having a good friend who is similar to your spouse really helps you to have a different perspective of your husband. If Deana or Barbara would do or say something that my husband would say, I could get a woman's perspective as to why they would react that way. This helps me to understand my husband more. The reverse is true with me being able to explain to them why their husband would say or do something. There have been countless times that Deana has called me because she was frustrated that her husband did something that she just didn't understand.

I remember one conversation when Deana was completely exasperated about something Marino, her husband, did. My response was "Wow, that was a great idea that Marino did that." It was definitely not the response she was looking for, but hearing my explanation of why he would take that action helped her understand him more. Barbara and I joke that she and Mike are twins due to their similarities. It's always a great thing when a friendship builds up your marriage!

I have another close friend, Janice, who has been one of my dearest friends for many years. She has three sons who have always been close to my youngest three sons. When my son, Dane, got married, Keith was his best man (and when Keith got married, Dane was his best man, also). The boys have maintained these friendships throughout the years, even though the MacDonald family moved away several years ago. A few years later we moved even farther away from their family. Recently, Dane moved to Virginia with his wife and two daughters near Janice and her boys. It's a blessing that they are able to be family to Dane and his family. Janice has this to say about her best friend,

My best friend is my rock. On days when I wasn't going to move out of bed, she would show up and get me going. We have stayed friends for the past 17 years now, and I thank God every day she was there to help me through. She was my support, and the one person I could call all hours of the night!

Not only has our family remained close to Janice and her family, but she has remained close to her best friend even after they moved far from each other. Janice knows that friendships take time and effort, especially with distance.

The same is true of my best friend, Deana. Even though we quickly became friends when we met, we only lived in the same city for a little over three years, and the rest of our friendship has been extremely long distance. First our family moved 10 hours away (which we thought was quite far). Six months later, her family moved to Germany where we couldn't visit each other at all due to finances and distance. Once again our families live 10 hours away. Compared to the overseas distance, it seems very close. I think this has also helped me deal with my sons living far away. Although the two that no longer live at home live on the East and West Coasts, respectively, at least I am able to visit them (though not as frequently as I would enjoy).

Some of my closest friends who I made while in Tennessee and also here in Texas are from YWAM *(Youth With a Mission)* and are not military-affiliated at all. My

association with these wonderful people started with my
friend, Asdrubal, who was a missionary from Costa Rica and
living in America as a pastor. He took Keir, my oldest son,
with him on a two month-long mission trip to Mexico, and
Keir became a part of the YWAM family. Mike was gone so
often that although Keir really wanted to do his DTS
(Discipleship Training Course) after high school in
Australia, he did it at the local base so that he could be closer
to me if I needed his help. That was a big sacrifice for Keir
that I have truly benefited from and appreciated in so many
ways. Not only did I have my son close to me when I needed
him, but I also gained many wonderful new friends through
him.

My YWAM friends really seem to understand the military
lifestyle of moving often and living in unfamiliar places,
because it is a lifestyle that they also live. They have always
been quick to call me, be there for me when I needed them
(if they were in the country), and (like the military
community) there are YWAM'ers all over the world. I was
so thrilled that when I moved here to Texas, it seemed that
many of the people with whom I became friends were either
in YWAM or had been in YWAM at one time.

I am truly blessed that God has put such wonderful people
in my life in all of the places that I've lived. I consider these
friends to be treasures that I hold dear to my heart. We
should never take for granted these people that God has put
strategically and specifically in our lives.

As wonderful as it is to have friends all over, there is a
loneliness that comes with being in the military that each
family member experiences: the soldier who is a Christian
and has few, if any, peers that share his convictions; the wife
who cannot make deep roots due to frequent moves and
whose husband may be gone often due to deployments or
training; the children who move to places where friendships
and groups are already established and feel like the *new kid,*
having to prove themselves yet again. Most of the residents
in the city where we now live have been here for
generations. The kids were born and raised here and have
life-long friends and relatives that live in the same city. My
sons don't even have first cousins, and all of our relatives

have lived thousands of miles away until we moved here closer to the West Coast. This has caused my sons to be very emotionally close to one another, although now that's not the case in proximity. But I have seen the struggles that my sons have had to go through to find a sense of belonging in a place that's already established.

Churches need to grasp this concept to better and reach out to those in their congregations who feel alone like this. Most military people will not admit this or even realize it, because it's a lifestyle they must live. But the church can offer comfort, hope, and a place where military families can feel loved and not alienated.

Although it's difficult for military wives to find true friendship, it's more difficult for a Christian who is in the military to find friendships that are not compromising and are actually uplifting. David says:

There aren't very many Christians where I work, if so, they are under cover. As far as my office, there are none that I would consider strong. There is one church-goer and possibly a couple other inconsistent Christmas/Easter Christians. My assumption is that they are not strong in their beliefs.

This is a difficult situation to be in for a soldier, because their fellow soldiers are those with whom they spend most of their time. When deployed overseas, David found often that he was limited in the number of Christians around him.

When I was at the bigger bases, there were Christians to fellowship with, but when out on the small teams, they are hard to come by. I've been on trips where I was the only Christian for months on end. Other times, I would start fellowship and Bible study groups or prayer groups. That would help, because it would bring closet Christians out, and it would be a chance to help build up believers or non-believers. For the most part, there are not a lot of Christians who are trying to walk out their walk in the military, especially when people are deployed. It seems like some believe it's a chance for them to let down their hair and forget about Christianity. Being a Christian in the military is lonely. You are very different if you try to walk a godly lifestyle. You definitely stand out and are different from everyone else. It's very hard, also, because things aren't as black-and-white as they are in church life. You must be very strong in your walk, because you are constantly challenged. There is a lot of opportunity to minister and plenty of chances to really make a difference in somebody's life. From what I've noticed, most people who go into the military have had some kind of church life in their past. Many are seeking meaning for their lives. It seems that many go crazy with sin, even those who seem to have a relationship with Christ. Then they get lost in their sins and really lose track of their lives.

Tips from Chapter 6

• Keeping any relationship thriving requires time and effort. Buy a box of blank cards and spend some time sending snail mail to friends out of town or even in your same city. Email could work, but an actual letter speaks loudly about your intentions as a friend.

• Help your kids keep in contact with their friends and encourage them in keeping their friendships thriving. Take time from your schedule to include their friends in events you are doing.

• Talk to your children about the importance of being a good friend. Luke 6:31 says *And just as you want them to do to you, you also do to them likewise.* Explain this concept of the Golden Rule to your children and how it applies to friendship also.

• Make a list of a few friends who live in your city, and brainstorm ways that you could help, encourage, or bless them.

Questions from Chapter 6

• Who are your best friends?

• Do you invest as much into your friendships as you should?

• Can you recall a time when a friendship went sour? Reflect on what you may have potentially done wrong so that you can learn to be a better friend.

• What are some ways that you can be a better friend to those you value and to those who might be lonely or feel isolated?

POINTS YOU WANT TO REMEMBER

feel free to jot down notes below...

Nicole Brocx Lee

POINTS YOU WANT TO REMEMBER
feel free to jot down notes below...

- C H A P T E R 7 -

Moving Mayhem

Now the Lord had said to Abram: Get out of your country, from your family and from your father's house, to a land that I will show you. I will make you a great nation; I will bless you and make your name great; and you shall be a blessing. I will bless those who bless you, and I will curse him who curses you; and in you all the families of the earth shall be blessed.

Genesis 12:1-3

No book written about military families would be complete without a section on moving. Moving is such an integral part of the military lifestyle. Moving has the potential to either make it appear that our world is crashing or that we are moving on to new and better things. The average frequency that a military family will move is about every three to four years. We have been fortunate that my husband's unit has allowed us to live in the same location for over 10 years. This has provided more stability for my children and has helped to establish more roots in the community.

I first moved to America from Holland with my family when I was just over two. Moving to another country as an immigrant often doesn't qualify one for many job opportunities. In Holland my dad had a good job, but these skills did not transfer over into the U.S. We moved often, based on job opportunities. The longest that my family had lived in one place was four years. This definitely prepared me for the many moves I would make as a military wife.

Our Family's Military Locations

While in the military, our family has moved five times.

This is not as many times as many military families have to move, considering we've been in the military for over 20 years. Due to the specialty of my husband's jobs, we have not had to live overseas. While he has spent much of his time overseas on various deployments and trainings, the rest of our family has been able to stay in the U.S. I have many friends who have fond memories of their times in other countries. This is an opportunity that the military provides and pays for, although many never have the privilege of taking advantage of it. Several friends of my friends have had the chance to travel all over Europe and/or Asia.

Mike and I met in Washington, then moved to California, and then back to Washington. From there we moved across the country to North Carolina, then Tennessee, and now we are western Texas. Although each of the states we've lived in are part of America, each location was completely different than the one before it. My husband and I spent both of our childhoods on the West Coast. As different as California and Washington are from each other, it was like moving to another country when we were deployed to the Deep South of North Carolina. I have found the saying *People are the same no matter where you live* to be completely inaccurate. Every place we have lived, the people in that place have a unique feel and flavor.

West Coast and East Coast Differences

The first obstacle we faced when moving from Washington to North Carolina was the language barrier. Yes, we all spoke English, but there was a vast difference between the West Coast dialect and the thick Southern accents. Eventually, we got used to the differences in the pronunciations and the words. Within a short amount of time North Carolina became home to us. We found a church where we felt welcomed and became very involved in the activities and with the congregation. We made many close friends that will remain our forever friends.

Our time there formed the foundation of our Christian faith. It was extremely difficult to move because we had mentors and close friends, people who helped us by showing us how to practically survive the difficult times in our lives by relying more on God than on how the circumstances around us appeared.

Separation and Loneliness

Tennessee was our next location, and it didn't seem as much like home to us as North Carolina did. One of the main reasons was Mike's long deployments. Less than six months after we moved to Tennessee, Mike went on a tour to Kosovo for the entire summer. A few months after he returned was the fateful day of September 11th, 2001. A few weeks after that he began his endless and long deployments to the Middle Eastern desert.

The season where we lived in Tennessee and Mike had his endless deployments was over ten years. Our sons were ages 4, 7, 9, and 13 when the deployments began. We could never have imagined what the next ten years of our lives would entail. If I would have known all that I would be doing and going through, I might have said *Count me Out!* But God has this great way of allowing us to only see a small portion of our lives at a time and not overwhelming us with the whole picture. Many times we ask God to show us everything, and it is by His great mercy that He allows us to see our lives in small portions: otherwise we would be overwhelmed.

Even though this was the longest period of time I had ever lived in one location (almost 11 years) it was the place and season of my life when I felt the most displaced and not at home. The fact that Mike was gone more than half of that time contributed to this feeling. When Mike was not overseas for the war, he was either in the country or overseas doing trainings. In addition, Tennessee was very different from where I had grown up, and it was foreign in every way to me.

Although North Carolina was a part of the South, I felt more at home while living there than in Tennessee due to close proximity of the ocean, the weather being more mild, and more outside activities to do. I did have friends in Tennessee, but most were not like the "family" I had in North Carolina. When your biological family is not near, it is important to have a church home that can be that family to you. Although we did have many friends, and the church claimed to be a family, it never gained that intimate level that a real family has. We did develop a few close family-like friends from the beginning of the time we lived there. But as they were military, they moved within a few years. I once spoke to a missionary friend of mine about how I did not understand how I could feel so lonely and not at home in a place where I know the Lord had sent our family. She explained that we are missionaries, and although God might cause us, via the military, to live in a specific location for many reasons, that doesn't necessarily mean that place will feel like home to us. I often remember her words of wisdom when I'm feeling detached and alone.

The Southwest

Nearly two years ago, we moved again. We are now in the Southwest. Although we are in Texas, it's so far west that it's more like we are living in New Mexico. We really are enjoying our time here. Two of our sons have moved out of the house, but we still have two boys living at home. This is definitely a new season in our lives. Mike's job is not at all similar to what he was doing while we lived in Tennessee. He is still in a position of leadership, but he does not currently deploy overseas and his schedule is not as erratic as it was. He does travel fairly often, but it is in the States and the times are very short compared to the separations we had to endure when we lived in Tennessee. We are extremely thankful to see him much more often, and we have a more normal family life.

Since moving here, we have made many new friends. Most are not in the military. It is quite fascinating to speak with people of all ages who have lived in the same place their whole lives. It's such a foreign concept to me and to many who live the military life. Since moving here, we've been helping with the teen youth group. Upon questioning them one day, I found that all but one was born and raised in this city. The one who wasn't is from East Texas! They are very interested and wide-eyed when we share with them our experiences, not only of living in other places but of the moves themselves.

Moving Helps for Military Families

When a family is getting ready to make a military move, known as a PCS (Permanent Change of Station), there are many factors they need to consider based on their family's needs. First of all, there are a few different options for moving. We have tried several of these methods that the military has available, and we have learned what does and does not work for us.

Complete Military Move

The first option (and this is the *only* option if you are moving overseas) is for the military to completely move your family and possessions. We have never used this method, because we have never moved overseas and were always trying to make money during our moves. For this option, no additional money is made, but everything is taken care of by the military. The amount of weight that is allowed for the soldier's household goods is based on the rank and number of dependents the military member has.

Do It Yourself

The second option is what is more commonly known as a *DITY* (Do-It-Yourself move). This is now termed the *Personally Procured Move Program*. With this type of move, the military member moves his/her own household goods, vehicles, etc. They rent their own moving trucks and do the move completely without the help of the military. What's the benefit of this? Money! Your family will be reimbursed for up to 100% of the Government Constructive Cost. This is usually far above the cost that it takes to move. You pay the costs upfront and get reimbursed after moving. As most people don't have the money to pay such large sums in advance, the military member is able to take an advance operating allowance to defray the costs of rental equipment, packing materials, etc.

It is important that the soldier visits the transportation department as soon as possible, makes an appointment, and tends to all paperwork. This process can take a considerable amount of time. Each situation varies considerably. If approval is not made in advance for the type of move that you are contemplating, it is possible that you will not be reimbursed for your move. The transportation department will also inform the soldier of all the options available and all details regarding the move. There is much to consider during a move such as the rental vehicle, the storage options for the location to where you will be moving, and possibly your current location. We had to rent two storage units and a large rental van during our last move because our home in Clarksville sold so quickly that we had to stay in a hotel for several weeks before my husband was scheduled to work in El Paso. It's extremely important to have all your paperwork, keep all the receipts needed for reimbursement in a safe and easy-to-access location, and keep track of the time limits for submitting all of the necessary papers to the right locations. It's a lot to remember: *a moving folder* for all of the information and important paperwork is a good idea.

With any move allow *more than enough time* for packing. If you are packing, make sure to have boxes, tape, markers, and all that you need in advance. Some stores will give you boxes if you ask. One store even had certain days of the week when they had stacks of empty boxes in the back of the store for use. We needed far more boxes than I imagined we would. Although I thought that we had prepared way in advance, it didn't turn out that way.

Our last move was a DITY move. I would still choose this route if we were to do it again, but there were many obstacles thrown our way during the move. The first inconvenience was actually a huge blessing. We put our house on the market, and it sold within one week. At this time we found out we had one week to completely move out and clean our house, because the new owners needed to be in that quickly. They were also a military family and needed to get into their house immediately, because the husband was deploying soon after they moved in.

The selling of our house happened so quickly, considering the state of the economy that caused many to be stuck for several years with homes they were trying to sell. It was surely a financial miracle. The scrambling around to move on such short notice was quite stressful. Thankfully our two boys who still live with us, Rainier and Theo, were a huge help. We have one good friend and his son who helped us move both into and out of our storage units, and from storage into the moving van. We had to find enough boxes to pack the belongings of six people. We packed up the house, moved everything into storage, cleaned our house, and moved into a hotel with no kitchen: all in *one* week. The one-room hotel became home to our family of four (plus our two pugs) for the next two weeks.

Partial DITY Move

The third option for moving is that the military transports the possessions, but the soldier and family drive to the new location in their own vehicles. This was formerly known as a Partial DITY Move. We chose this option for two of our moves, as we had four young children and my father-in-law living with us. The military contracts out movers to come to the house, pack up all the belongings, and move everything to the new location. This option is much easier than moving everything yourself, but there are downfalls to it.

A negative aspect of this type of move is that someone is moving your items, and they usually don't care about them as much as you do. The movers are not military and are contracted out to the lowest bidder. So most times they are not using the utmost care when handling your possessions. In both moves, items were broken and damaged. Even though you can claim these items to get reimbursement, most often the amount of money is not enough to cover the damages. If it is something of sentimental value, it is irreplaceable. We have only had minor things broken, but I have had several friends with major amounts of damage to their things.

The saddest situation I have heard regarding a move, happened to our friends. Our friends noticed that the boxes looked different than when they were packed and that what was in the boxes did not correlate to the boxes' labels. Many items were missing, and they lost family heirlooms that were never replaced. If one must do a Partial DITY move, make sure to personally pack breakables and family keepsakes and keep them in the personal vehicle.

The Partial DITY option is what we used for one of our moves, because it involved four, young sons and a long distance. One huge thing is to make sure there is no more weight than allotted. You do make more money depending upon how much your personal possessions weigh. However, if they are over the amount allotted, *you* may end up paying. When we moved from the West Coast to the East Coast with our four sons and Mike's dad, we thought that we would be way under the allotted weight limit (we didn't have too many possessions). We did not consider the weight of his dad's things, but simply had the movers pack them up and move them. When we arrived at our destination, we had to pay well over $1,000 because we were over the weight limit. To add to the frustration, we found that Mike's dad's "prized possessions" were mainly old magazines, rusted tools and other trash items! We definitely learned an expensive lesson there!

A woman who is an acquaintance recently moved across the country and discovered some problems when their household goods finally arrived:

Well, my furniture is here, but so far the damages are tremendous! The trunk is badly damaged. My son's mattress is nowhere to be found, the couch is damaged and several other items, and we haven't even begun on the boxes yet!

This is unfortunately a common occurrence. A helpful hint is to take photos of your items before the move so that you can better document them when making a claim if they get damaged. Before and after pictures of the damaged item gives an easier and more accurate assessment of the damage.

The second item of extreme importance in a move where others are packing your items is when you are watching them as they pack your items. *This is crucial.* As you can see in the prior moving mishap, it still is not a guarantee that your possessions will arrive in the same condition as when they were packed. However, it does give you more of a chance of controlling *how* items are packed. We discovered that near the end of the day when we were not paying as much attention to how they packed, the movers stuck everything in boxes marked *Garage.* This was so frustrating as we tried to smoothly unpack!

Because my husband has been in the military for over 23

years, we have moved several times. Because of the kinds of units with which he deploys, we have never PCS'd (Permanent Change of Station) overseas. But we have moved to several locations within the country. We have been able (not always conveniently so) to travel all across the United States and back again. In fact, our military moves have almost consisted of a complete circle of the country!

Each of the moves had obstacles of some sort. Our last move was the most difficult and stressful because we had to move quickly and had issues with the moving van. The move was 1,300 miles, and the military gave us the allotted five days. We planned to drive a about five hours a day, relax at the hotel pool in late afternoon, and give our pugs a break from being in the car. *Our plans fell flat literally.* We wound up having four blown tires on four separate days of our travels. Not only that, but twice the engine wouldn't start on the moving van! By the time someone came to change the van's tire and we got to the hotel each day, it was already past dinner-time, and we had just enough energy to grab some food and go to sleep. We finally arrived at our house at 11:45 p.m. just 15 minutes shy of July 4th. It felt like paradise! It's understandable that I'm hoping that we don't have to move anytime in the near future.

Overseas Move

Since we have never lived overseas, I asked several friends who have to share their experiences. Each of them had a different view about living overseas.

Gabby is a young wife who moved overseas with her husband fairly soon after they got married. Most of what Gabby had to say was extremely positive, and she has really made the most of her time overseas by taking advantage of all of the experiences that were available to her.

Most of the countries I have been to, I can get away with not knowing much about their language and feel safe and can navigate; a smartphone always helps, too. My limited speaking abilities have never been much of a hindrance; signing goes a long way. Meeting people from all over the world helps me understand what is truly American about myself and makes me reassess why I do what I do, and if it truly is beneficial not only to me but the world.

Driving is not too scary. Roundabouts are now fun and make a lot more sense. Driving on the left side of the road is not that big of a deal at all. I refuse to be egocentric and say 'wrong side of the road' like so many Americans do. We are not the last say on what side of the road to drive on.

Many of the wives have become close friends. I know I will have their friendship for my lifetime. Being overseas, there is not time to waste and people tend to be more transparent and great relationships form. I have been sick and not able to call my husband for help because he was TDY or deployed and my girlfriends would come and take care of me. I have driven friends and been driven to the ER several times because my husband was away. It's nice knowing that there are people who God has placed in your life to act as family for the time being. Also, being that family for someone when they are in need is a great feeling. Traveling with my friends has been so amazing. It is one of the best experiences of being overseas. I feel really safe over here and recommend that people go on several trips with some girl friends or just find one good friend to go on trips with. It's been worth every penny spent. Seeing the concentration camps in Poland, going on a mission trip in Romania with the youth group I volunteer in, running from Marathon to Athens into the original Olympic stadium was epic, and taking a train trip across Italy to see the David and the Vatican. Those are only a few of the blessings I have been able to experience living over here. The schools are great and there is a great sense of community. It's homeschool-friendly: a lot of home schoolers can opt to play on the sports teams. For high school away games, kids will bus to other countries!

A Bible verse that Gabby sees applicable to her life overseas experiences is Psalm 68:6a. She said she has claimed this promise regarding family: *God sets the solitary in families.* This has also been one of my favorite verses for many reasons, because it's fitting for the military community and those who move often. Churches need to be the family we need when biological families are too far away. Church should be functioning as a family and not just a location to meet.

One of the biggest stressors to a marriage and family is moving. But with preparation and organization many of the hassles and problems can be avoided. There will always be unforeseen obstacles in anything we go through, but having all of the knowledge and information will prevent much of the stress in the moves that are so much a part of military life.

Tips from Chapter 7

• Before you move, have a file to keep all of your receipts, paperwork, and anything pertaining to your move on hand and readily accessible at all times.

• Line up services way in advance that you may need: childcare, hotels, realtors.

• Keep in mind that with the military things can change quickly, and your time schedule needs to be as flexible as possible.

• Read through the life of Abraham in the Old Testament of the Bible, and see how he had to move his family often. Read how what he did was in obedience to God and how he was blessed through it: not only for himself and his family, but also for generations to follow. See if you can find stories of other people who have had similar, nomadic lifestyles.

Questions from Chapter 7

• What have you learned from the moves you've experienced, and what would you do differently?

• Do you know someone who is going to move? Offer them help in a specific way. Often if someone is asked for help in general, they could be so overwhelmed that they can't even think of what they need. If you ask someone if they need help packing, sorting, or babysitting, it will be easier for them to receive the help.

• How do your children feel about an upcoming move you may have to go through? Have you spoken to them in detail and helped them to see how this move can be an exciting and fun experience for them? After you have moved, are you helping them to readjust and also keep in contact with their friends?

POINTS YOU WANT TO REMEMBER

feel free to jot down notes below...

- C H A P T E R 8 -

Parenting

And these words which I command you today shall be in your heart. You shall teach them diligently to your children, and shall talk of them when you sit in your house, when you walk by the way, when you lie down, and when you rise up.

Deuteronomy 6:6-7

Parenting is such a touchy subject. On one hand, people don't want to be told how to raise their children. On the other hand, it seems that almost all parents need direction in this area. My sons were never perfect angels, and there were countless incidents where it would have been easier to pretend they weren't mine due to their behavior. I do not think that children should be ruling the home, and that parents should expect their children to raise themselves. This appears to be the society we live in today.

One major key to helping your household run more smoothly is structure. In the military family, this is something that is even more important and more difficult to obtain. There is so much change going on in the military household due to moves and deployments that is it important that you really add structure to the areas of their lives: structures that you are able to control. When there is structure and there are boundaries in your children's lives, they feel more secure that things are under control.

Being a Single Mom

When I was a kid there was an animated sitcom by Hanna-Barbera called *Wait Till Your Father Gets Home,* inspired by the series *All in the Family.* It was mainly adult humor that I didn't understand at the time, yet I still loved to watch it. It aired for two years. And although I don't remember much about the show (because the comedy was beyond my understanding), I do remember the theme song quite well.

The premise of the movie is that when the kids acted up, the mom would threaten the children that she would tell their dad when he got home and they would really get in trouble. Of course, the mom should be disciplining and correcting throughout the day, but there is always that healthy fear of the father that would cause the children to want to behave due to repercussions! When the dad is deployed, this disciplinary option or addition can *never* effectively be used. It's just not effective when you tell the kids "Wait for nine months till your dad gets home, and you'll really get in trouble!" It's up to the mother to be consistent and quick to discipline. If she lets these things slide, the behaviors will only escalate.

I have seen this in my own children. They know when I'm not in control: when their environment is chaotic. Children will push their limits, but in reality they only want to be given boundaries. They may seem to resist and may even voice that things are not fair, but in the end they feel more safe and secure knowing that they are cared enough to provide them with stability.

As parents we need to remember that we are the ones in charge of our children's safety and protection. They can argue their point all they want, but in the end it is our obligation to provide them with the safest and most stable environment so that they can fulfill all that God has for them.

When the husband is deployed, one of the most difficult things for the mom is disciplining the children. When you are the sole parent at home, it seems much easier to keep the peace by giving into every want that the child has. Of course, it is important that you provide for their needs, but fulfilling every want is not beneficial for them.

The primary goal in parenting is not to make your children happy. The goal is to teach them, by word and by example, how to be loving, giving and emotionally stable adults who are able to make a positive impact in this world.

An adult who has been taught from childhood to only seek pleasure for himself or herself would be hedonistic: someone whose main focus is the pursuit of pleasure and self-gratification. A child with these behaviors would be considered a brat, and we, as parents, need to not encourage them in this area *not* to turn out that way.

Consistency and Routine

Disciplining your children with consistency is not an easy task, but the security that you provide for your children with consistent discipline is something that will profit both your family as a whole and your children personally. The results will be well worth all the time and effort. As with anything, your main motive should be love. We should love our children and want what is best for them, not because it's easier for us but because we care about them enough to take the time to train them up in the way that's the most beneficial.

Provide your children with routine as much as you're able. This doesn't mean that you need to structure their every waking moment. But as much as you're able, try to stay consistent with a schedule. If they know what to expect and when to expect it, things will run more smoothly for you and it will provide more stability for your children. It's similar to having rules and boundaries for children so that they feel more secure when they know what to expect and what is expected of them.

It's not easy being a parent, and being a military spouse makes parenting even more of a challenge. Why? Because we must redouble effort, redouble spousal communication, and have routines B and C in place *when* routine A falls apart. Because our children cannot rationalize like adults can, we have to set, reset, and maintain the attitude and climate of their environment. If we are fearful and complaining all the time, our children will replicate that and often magnify our emotional state. If we are able to keep a climate of peace in our households, then our children will be more content and less fearful. If we heap fear and anxiety on our children while they are young, they can carry this into their adulthood. The Bible says that the only thing that is good to fear is God himself. As for fearing anything else, Isaiah 41:10 says *Do not fear, for I am with you; do not be dismayed, for I am your God. I will strengthen you and help you; I will uphold you with my righteous right hand.* And again in Isaiah 41:13 *For I am the Lord, your God, who takes hold of your right hand and says to you, Do not fear; I will help you.*

Time With Your Children is Important

Remember that each child is different, and something that may help in the adjustment of someone else's children might not work for your child. The same holds true for your individual children.

We have 4 children. Although each is male, they are all completely different from one another. One is creative and artsy, one is very structured and precise, one is completely out of the box, and one is a combination of all of the above! None is better than the other, just different. They each have their own gifts, and they each have ways that they cope with the struggles of military life.

It's up to us parents to find out what the best solution for our children is in each situation that they are in. This comes with much prayer and much time spent with our children, both collectively and individually. Our children's number one need is our time. As much as quality spent with our children is important, this is even more important in a military family with one spouse gone often. We are not able to compensate for our spouse being away, but we can and need to be there for our children. This often means that we are not able to do the things that we may want to do when we want to do them. Remember that *we* are the parents and the adults. Our children need to know that they are our top priority! The time that we pour into our children when they are young will be greatly rewarded when they are older. Proverbs 22:6 says *Train up a child in the way he should go, and when he is old he will not depart from it.*

Keep Their Father in the Children's Minds

My friend, Janice, is one of the most wonderful mothers who I have consistently observed in action. I'm not just saying this because she is a good friend of mine, but she was always so thoughtful in keeping her sons informed of their dad's actions and whereabouts. I remember vividly this great idea that she implemented for her sons:

Garth deployed for Iraq the beginning of 2003 for 15 months and then in 2005 for 12 months. We always made a wall in our home (Dad's wall). It had a map showing where he was, and then any photos sent were hung around it. It was a great way to keep our boys' spirits up. Every place Garth went was marked by a star.

Even with all the planning and doing what we can to make sure our children understand where their dads are, we still have to contend with our children's emotions. Just as our own emotions can go haywire from all the changes and challenges of being a military wife, we need to realize that our children will not only be fueled by our emotions but will add in their own emotional turmoil. Once again, we can either react based on their emotions or we can stop and assess the situation. Not every time they lash out emotionally will be an act of rebellion. It is really a fine balance to show sympathy and grace on our children when they are going through something that is really difficult and when they don't know how to handle their emotions. We need to be willing to allow our children to feel comfortable speaking to us and knowing that we are listening to them. This communication is vital to our children and to their relationship with you and with the Lord. The way our children relate to God will often mirror their relationship with us. My boys range in ages from 17 to 26. Two are living in other locations, and it was been heartbreaking to me when they moved out because they are such a huge part of my life. I strongly believe the friendships I have with my sons stem from much time poured into them in their younger years.

Balancing Our Time as a Parent

Many parents don't realize that there is a season for everything in our lives. We listen to what others tell us we should do. We watch movies where the heroes seem to be doing everything they want and accomplishing everything they set out to do. It's definitely good to have goals in life and to strive to accomplish the things that God has called us to do, but it's another thing to place unreasonable expectations upon ourselves. Parenting is one of the areas where it is so easy to use comparisons and to dictate what we *should* be doing and how we should be raising our children.

As with everything, balance is key. Parenting in itself is difficult and challenging. In the case of a military family one parent is often not home, so balancing our lives can be even more challenging. When the husband is often gone, we need to realize that we are the ones carrying the primary weight of parenting. If we are gone much of the time, having our child in childcare long hours every day and putting our needs and the needs of others before the needs of our own children will cause our families to suffer. We don't need to become hermits in your houses with our children. But because we are the sole parent on hand, we need to realize that our children need our presence even more.

When my husband deployed, I had the tendency to be *too* busy. I wanted to keep myself occupied and make the time go by more quickly. Not only did I wear myself out, but my sons also suffered because of it. The more deployments that my husband went through, the more I realized this and tried to cut back on commitments that did not benefit our family. Through the years I have learned that I don't need to be accomplishing something major to be effective in parenting. Time spent with our children is time spent wisely.

Often those around us will assume that we have more free time with our husbands gone. If they are not in the same circumstance that we are in, they don't often realize all that we are going through. We must not let others pressure us into doing more than we know we can handle. Guarding the time spent with our children is important, first and foremost.

Rebecca's Story

Although it was difficult for Rebecca when she was younger and her father was often gone, she is fortunate to have a family that saw the importance of being there for one another:

When dad wasn't at home, it was very tough on me. Not that it wasn't for my mom and sister, but I was and still am a daddy's girl. He and I have truly similar personalities. It was always just easier when he was around. As far as my role in the family, it never really changed. I was and always have been the baby. My job was to be in distress as often as possible so someone could come to my rescue. That's a joke, of course. Although I wasn't actually able to take and handle myself until I made it into my teens, most of the time my dad or sister fought my battles for me. For awhile my parents were worried that I wouldn't be a strong enough person to stand against things like peer pressure and 'whatnot', but they saw as I got older that I was taking after my sister in that I wouldn't put up with some people's nonsense. After being raised by three very strong, tough people, I've developed a few traits after them.

Rebecca was truly blessed to grow up in a home where quality and quantity time were stressed. This is not the case with many families. It is saddening to witness children going through these difficult times, needing their parents' time, and not getting it. Often, when these children are older, they will rebel and not want so much to do with their families.

Parenting is one of the most difficult but, also, most rewarding jobs. Our children are an extension of us, and there is no greater heritage that we can offer to the world than our children. *Behold, children are a heritage from the Lord, the fruit of the womb is a reward. Like arrows in the hand of a warrior, so are the children of one's youth. Happy is the man who has his quiver full of them; they shall not be ashamed, but shall speak with their enemies in the gate.* Psalm 127: 3-5.

My prayer is that we would remember that our children are our heritage, and that we would view them as arrows that we shoot out farther than we could ever go by ourselves.

Tips from Chapter 8

• Make a calendar of how you spend your time and note how much time is allotted for just you and your children. If you haven't put aside as much time as you think you have for your children, take some things out of your schedule and actively schedule time for them.

• Write a note to each of your children individually and put it in a prominent place that they will notice. Ask them on a date in the note for a lunch or movie of their choice. Dates with our children are a wonderful tradition.

• Write a list for each of your children and the things that are special about each. Write down things that they need to improve on and pray about both of these areas.

Questions from Chapter 8

• What are some things that you do that are pulling you away from being with your children? Can you find a way to better balance our time?

• What activities can you add to your schedule that will be fun for both you and your children? Can you find a way to make these activities possible?

• How can you help a family whose husband may be gone? Could you help the wife with chores she needs to get done so that she can have more time pouring into her children or something comparable.

POINTS YOU WANT TO REMEMBER

feel free to jot down notes below...

- CHAPTER 9 -

Pre-deployment: Preparation Is Key

To everything there is a season, a time for every purpose under heaven.

Ecclesiastes 3:1

In the next three chapters I will explain what it means for a soldier to be deployed, and I'll describe the periods of time both before and after the deployment. It would be easy to lump them all into a *deployment* chapter, but each aspect of this process is unique. Looking through the dictionary, I came across several meanings for the military use of the word *deploy: 1. To adopt or cause to adopt a battle formation, esp. from a narrow fro formation. 2. To position troops in readiness for combat. 3. To bring forces into action.*

What Were you doing 9/11?

For a military wife sometimes the just reaction to the word *deployment* can bring forth roller-coaster ride of emotions. Before September 11th, the word *deployment* meant that the soldier was going to be gone for awhile (often to another country) and would be doing something for our country. The sense that harm or even worse could occur so that the husband could possibly not come home was most often *not* on anyone's mind. Now, when we hear the word *deployment,* our minds start reeling because we are aware of all that this will usually entail.

If we are old enough, most of us can remember exactly where we were and what we were doing that fateful morning of September 11, 2001. My family had just moved to Tennessee with our four sons (ages 4, 7, 8 and 12) less than a year prior to this. We were in our first house that we owned, and my husband had recently come home from being gone the entire summer (almost four months) to Kosovo, which at the time I thought was a really a long time to be away from us. As much as we didn't want to move from our last location, we were excited about this new season and all that God had for us in this new location. Little did I know how these plans would be drastically changed and so suddenly.

On the morning of September 11th my friend, Janice, called me to tell me what she had just seen on the news. She was aware that I had no cable television, and would need updates on anything important like tornadoes (common in our area) and world events. And what shocking information she gave me! For me, personally, this meant a huge change in my life. I had just sent out newsletters the prior week for a missions trip that I was planning on being part of to Thailand. I was excited to go and was getting ready to get my passport. The mission trip was postponed until flights were available and safe. I felt that God was specifically conveying to me that this was not my season to be doing things like this for many reasons.

First of all, just a few weeks after 9/11, my husband was gone to Afghanistan on his first deployment. I really feel that it is important for our kids to have stability in their lives. If both of the parents are leaving, I don't feel that provides stability at all. It's difficult enough for children to comprehend what is going on when one family member leaves for an extended period of time. But if both of us were to go, that would have had me putting my wants and desires in front of their needs as children. Mike was gone on deployments or trainings constantly, I was homeschooling the children, and we had no family nearby who could watch them if I did go. Those were enough reasons to have me stay.

How did 9/11 affect us on a national level? What exactly happened on September 11, 2001 that changed that course of our country and the lives of so many military families?

September 11, 2001

The following is from a website called *WISE GEEK*. They

are a team of researchers, writers, and editors, dedicated to providing short, clear and concise answers to common questions on the web. Currently, there are over 200 active contributors. The following description of what happened on 9/11 seems quite accurate, and I feel it is important that we remember what happened in the past, so that we can be aware of why we are doing what we are doing now as a country. So many are quick to forget.

September 11, 2001 was a bright, crisp morning in many regions of the United States, which was shattered when the nation was attacked by terrorists. Americans and friends all over the world remember where they were and what they were doing that fateful Tuesday morning, when the first attack commenced with a plane being flown into the World Trade Center in New York.

On September 11, 2001 at 8:46 a.m. Eastern time, American Airlines Flight 11 was flown into the north tower of the World Trade Center. At first, many believed the event to be an accident, simple pilot error. The news of the crash preempted many regular programs as cameramen and photographers captured flames, billowing smoke, and sadly, bodies of people who plunged to their deaths rather than remaining trapped in the building. As journalists and everyday people continued filming, snapping photos, and watching the skies, another plane, United Airlines Flight 175, was flown into the south tower at 9:02 a.m. America was clearly under attack.

Before people could absorb the shock, another strike was being executed. Unbeknownst to Americans, at least one more plane headed toward Washington, D.C. At 9:37 a.m., American Airlines Flight 77 was flown into the Pentagon, the headquarters of America's military operations. People were horrified to learn that other planes that may have been hijacked were still not accounted for. Loved ones of passengers on United Airlines Flight 93 began receiving phone calls, learning that the flight had indeed been hijacked. They told their loved ones of the earlier attacks.

The brave men and women on Flight 93 refused to let their plane or their deaths be used to hurt America. They died as heroes, as they retook the plane, crashing it into a field near Shanksville, Pennsylvania instead of allowing the hijacked plane to go on to its intended target, believed to be nearby Washington, D.C. It was 10:03 on September 11, 2001.

In less than one and a half hours, three American landmarks had been hit and one had been narrowly avoided. Soon, U.S. Airspace was closed down completely. Many believe that other attacks were still pending on September 11 and that this unprecedented move by the U.S. government thwarted further atrocities.

America learned a lot about heroes on September 11, 2001. First responders, including police officers, firefighters, paramedics, and a host of off duty responders, construction workers, medical professionals, and everyday people risked their lives to help evacuate as many people as possible from the burning and badly damaged Twin Towers, as well as from the Pentagon. Brave men and women lost their lives on September 11, along with the victims inside each building and aboard each plane.

Many sayings are associated with the September 11 atrocities, such as, 'We will never forget.' Certainly, Americans will never forget the day that thousands of innocent people, their parents, siblings, children, spouses, and friends, were murdered on American soil. September 11 is also known as 'the day the United States once again became united' and 'the day the world changed.' It's true that Americans banded together to help each other through the harrowing events and the aftermath of that day. It's also true that the world reacted to the September 11, 2001 attack, and perhaps the world did change.

Americans were touched by the heartfelt sentiments and condolences shared by citizens and leaders from over one hundred other nations. Hearing the National Anthem played in other countries brought fresh tears to the eyes of many. The tributes and kindnesses were without measure, and they helped America face the atrocities of September 11, as well as the taunts of her enemies, who danced in the streets and celebrated the brutal deaths of nearly 3,000 Americans in an unprovoked and unprecedented attack.

While some believe that U.S. foreign policy played a hand in inciting these attacks, they were not acts of self-defense, nor is there any way to justify such tactics. The attacks of September 11, 2001 were executed mainly against civilians, and they were nothing less than atrocities, carried out by terrorist extremists.

Have We Forgotten?

It's interesting to note that one of the quotes of that day was *We will never forget.* But it seems that as a people and a country, we seemed to have forgotten this matter so quickly. I did find that people suddenly became extremely patriotic with flags flying everywhere, and signs up that said *God bless America.* And America was supportive of the President's goal of taking down the terrorists on their own soil to prevent this from happening on American ground. As a country, our people were all for getting the bad guys. I found that in the military town where I lived not less than a month after everyone was rallied around for such a cause, the flags were coming down, the patriotic signs were removed, and they were all replaced with the next holiday adornment: Halloween. My husband was in Afghanistan before Halloween, so my thoughts and heart were definitely still focused on squashing terrorism. My husband was the only one from our church who was deployed.

How quickly we forget if we are not directly involved! It wasn't until others in our church started to deploy, several months later, that I actually felt that people had compassion. As this is not something that had occurred at such a magnitude before, *people just didn't know how to react or what to do.*

After more families had husbands that deployed, a ministry started up in the church to help the military families of those whose husbands were gone. The only problem with that was that *it was led by a military spouse whose husband was deployed!* And why is this a bad thing, you may ask? It was bad because this woman (who was and still is a good friend of mine) needed people to pour into *her* to help *her* out. As much as she had the heart to help other women in her situation, it would have been much more healthy to her emotions and spiritual battles if she could have been a participant and helper in this ministry and *not* the main leader. Also, it was not something that she volunteered to lead but that she was asked by church leadership to do! This was a great ministry that helped many in the church. Because it was led and run by the military spouses whose husbands were deployed, however, it didn't last long due to burnout.

This is *exactly* what happened in the church that we attended and became very involved in following the prior church. This time it was *I* who started and led the wives' ministry. I had set it up so that I would lead it, but I would have the help and support of other leaders in the church who were not military. My main co-leader was Tabitha, whose husband was not in the military, but who was also so wonderful in helping, doing every thing I asked her to do, giving input, and filling in on the areas where I was weaker. She was such a wonderful help to me and all to the women to whom we ministered. Still, it was more than what we could handle by ourselves. The wives ministry grew, and it was much more than we could bear on just our shoulders, because I knew that with my husband deployed so often that it would just not be possible without it being a huge strain on my family and my emotional health. Unfortunately, I may not have conveyed my intent quite the way I needed to convey it, because it turned out that the ministry was completely on my shoulders. I would get the pat on the back, and the we-are-praying-for-you moments, but this was not enough help to run such a huge ministry as this. I had to let this ministry fold, because it was becoming more of a burden for me. I do believe that a military wives ministry is a wonderful and necessary tool, but for a spouse whose husband is often away (especially if she has children)... this is too much of a stretch.

There are many aspects to the kind of deployment where your spouse is overseas for an extended period of time, fighting for your country. My husband has now participated in seven combat deployment since 9/11. We have been through enough deployments to know that while each deployment is not easier than the one before, at least experience has taught us that we know what we can expect.

The first aspect of the deployment cycle is *pre-deployment*. This generally starts the month prior to your husband's departure, but it can occur well before that.

The pre-deployment period can easily become a roller coaster ride of emotions. So many things are running through the head of every member of the family. The husband is often preoccupied with getting ready for what he will be doing overseas. He can easily become distracted, because he is focusing on his upcoming missions. It's very easy for the wife to feel like she is being pushed away. The husband may also be subconsciously distancing himself: this is very common. At the same time the wife can often become clingy and more emotional. So we have the husband being more distant and the wife being more clingy. This can be a disaster if both sides are not aware of what is going on with their emotions. As a wife, you need to step back and realize that this is not a personal attack. It's a coping mechanism on the husband's part, but he is also very busy getting everything together for his upcoming deployment. You will make life easier on your husband if you can not take everything he does and says personally. I know: that's easier said than done!

Preparing for Deployment

Some practical things to prepare for deployment are legal documents: the will, Power of Attorney, medial papers, tax information, and anything else you need to get done while your husband is at home. For some things you will need a specialized Power of Attorney, so make sure you have all of what you need before your husband is overseas. You will also need to fill out a paper that explains what you must do in case something happens to your husband. As much as you do not want to even think about the fact that your husband could get injured or die, it's something that *must* be done. In this document you will list your children, who you want notified in case of death, your religion, and even the care for your pets. If this paper is not filled out, then the needs you may have and the people you would want notified might not ever happen.

It's also very important to go to any pre-deployment

meetings that your husband's unit may have. It's easy to complain about the FRG (Family Readiness Groups) and what they *aren't* doing or *should be* doing, but remember that these groups consist of volunteers who are there to help you. These meetings will provide you with needed information like contact persons, what to do if you have an emergency, different resources you could use, when your husband leaves and is scheduled to return, etc. If you do not go to these meetings, it will be much more difficult to get the information needed. I have had several women complain to me that they don't know what's going on in their husband's unit, and it is often based on the fact that they did not go to the meetings that were set up to help them obtain this information.

Pre-deployment is a time of planning. It can be a time to let fear set in, but remember not to allow fear to get the upper hand. In planning you are preparing yourself both physically and emotionally for what may occur while your spouse is deployed. Let your friends and family know that your husband will be gone and that you will probably need their help while he is away. At the same time, do not expect people to understand what we are going through. Also, do not take offense when they are not helping like you think they should. Remember that even though we are going through the difficult times, people who are not going through what you are cannot fully comprehend.

As Christians we should all rally around each other to help, but that is not always the case. Ask people in advance for phone numbers of people who you can go to with automotive issues, house repairs, heating and air conditioning, and anything that you may need while your husband is gone. It's easier to prepare in advance than go through a crisis scrambling! In the same manner, don't expect everyone to do everything for you. If you are asking for a repair need, be fair in the amount of money that you are willing to pay. People know when they are being taken advantage of and taken for granted. But *don't* let your needs stop you from asking for help.

Make the Most of Your Time Together

Clear your calendar so that you can spend as much time together with one another, both as a family *and* as a couple. Include the children as much as possible, but make sure you are able to spend time as a couple also. Make sure those last days are spent just with your family, and not with extended family or friends. This is time that should be reserved and made special for you and yours only. Guard your time together. At the same time, try not to continually spend money like a crazy person and get yourself into a debt that you will have to work hard to pay off. You probably will be going out to eat more often and doing things that require money, but try to keep your finances under control.

Prepare your children for your husband's deployment. Explain to them how long he will be gone, and give a brief description of why he will be there. Build him up in their eyes so that they will look up to him and see that he is there for a purpose. Remember that you set the tone for the peace that is in your household. Look up information about where he will be (if you are able to know that in advance), and pray with your children and your husband. Encourage communication between your husband and your children during this pre-deployment time. Don't push the issue, but encourage it. The children can often feel pushed aside during this time, but you need to make sure that they do not feel that way.

Another aspect people don't realize is that for most deployed soldiers, the availability of chaplains during deployments is very limited. David, who has traveled the world to various locations understands this:

Chaplains can't be everywhere. There are small bases that don't have them, because there is only one Chaplain per Battalion (Army). There are normally four Companies in each Battalion and three to four Platoons in each Company. So it, it's very hard for them to cover down on (or be assigned to) everyone. Often units are broken up and assigned to different areas. It's not always safe for these Chaplains to get to all the segments. As far as being spiritual guides: I have had some really good Chaplains, but I have also had some very weak (spiritually speaking) Chaplains. Although I've never had one, a Chaplain can be a Mormon or Muslim. They may be nice people, but I wouldn't call them spiritual guides.

It's important for military families to realize the minimal availability of a chaplain before their spouse leaves for a deployment. If the couple is having any struggles in their marriage before the spouse deploys, it would be best for their marriage if they could get the help they need before the soldier is gone. He will most often not have the spiritual help that he needs while he is overseas.   It is also important for people in the church to understand this, so that they can better help those who are getting ready to deploy. As much as we'd like this period of time before the husband deploys to be just a time for having fun activities, it's vital that important matters be taken care of before the spouse leaves, as they can tend to be magnified while the couple is separated from one another.

As with anything involving preparation, plan more than enough time to take care of all the needs that you have. If you have marital needs, thinking that you can begin counseling for deep issues isn't very wise to start a week before your husband is deployed. Plan wisely, and you will save yourself a lot of wasted time and heartache. Being unnecessarily worried in advance about something is completely different than planning wisely.

Tips from Chapter 9

• If you know a family who has a member planning on deploying, tell them that you are available for whatever they would need to help, and be specific about it: babysitting, fixing minor things (only if you're able to!), mowing lawns, spending time listening.

• If your spouse is getting ready to deploy, try to slow down not only your schedule but also in your mind as you prepare for this separation. Realize that your emotions can be going haywire, and try not to be controlled by your feelings.

• If your spouse is deploying, go through everything that you need well ahead of time (paperwork, back up repairmen etc.). It's much less stressful to be prepared in advance than having to scramble the last few days you have together. Try to make the end of the time as peaceful as you possible are able.

Questions from Chapter 9

• If you've gone through the deployment cycle before, what are some things that you did that you regret and could learn from? What could you have done differently?

• Of your military family and friends, do you know if any will be deploying in the future? What can you do to help make things go more smoothly for them? Have you done what you can to help them?

• Can you think of scenarios that could come up while your spouse is deployed that you are not able to handle while he is gone? Talk these situations over with your husband, but not in a fearful way.

• Plan for backup help. Are you finding that you and your family are in a frenzy with everything going on physically and emotionally? Take the time to communicate your thoughts and fears.

POINTS YOU WANT TO REMEMBER
feel free to jot down notes below...

Nicole Brocx Lee

POINTS YOU WANT TO REMEMBER

feel free to jot down notes below...

- CHAPTER 10 -

Deployment: Ignorance Is Not Bliss!

Get wisdom! Get Understanding!

Proverbs 4:5

Do Our Beliefs Matter?

It's important that we know what our husbands are fighting for so that we are able to take ownership of that information and support them more specifically. We need to be prepared to answer those friends and family members who may not support what our spouses are doing. Without taking offense, we need to be prepared to answer their questions in a way that will support our husbands. We must educate ourselves about what is going on in the world. World events are all tied together, and we need to know what is happening around the world.

What is a Biblical world view, and why is it important to have a Biblical worldview as our solid foundation? *The Barna Group, Ltd.* (which includes its research division, *The Barna Research Group)* is a private, non-partisan, for-profit organization that conducts primary research on a wide range of issues and products, produces resources pertaining to cultural change, leadership and spiritual development, and facilitates the healthy spiritual growth of leaders, children, families and Christian ministries. Located in Ventura, California, *Barna* has been conducting and analyzing primary research to understand cultural trends related to values, beliefs, attitudes and behaviors since 1984. This *George Barna* survey examines changes in worldview among Christians over the past 13 years:

For the purposes of the survey, a 'biblical worldview' was defined as believing that absolute moral truth exists; the Bible is totally accurate in all of the principles it teaches; Satan is considered to be a real being or force, not merely symbolic; a person cannot earn their way into Heaven by trying to be good or do good works; Jesus Christ lived a sinless life on earth; and God is the all-knowing, all-powerful creator of the world who still rules the universe today. In the research, anyone who held all of those beliefs was said to have a biblical worldview. Overall, the current research revealed that only 9% of all American adults have a biblical worldview.

Ongoing research by The Barna Group on these matters consistently demonstrates the powerful impact a person's worldview has on their life. A worldview serves as a person's decision-making filter, enabling them to make sense of the complex and huge amount of information, experiences, relationships and opportunities they face in life. By helping to clarify what a person believes to be important, true and desirable, a worldview has a dramatic influence on a person's choices in any given situation.

It's peculiar to me how many Americans consider themselves to be Christian, yet only a small percentage have a biblical worldview and actually know what it is to be a Christian. It's important that you know what you believe and why you believe it. It's just not wise to follow the leading of others if you don't know *what* you are following, and more importantly why you are following it. We should all periodically ask ourselves if we believe and evaluate how we act upon those beliefs. People will live out what they truly believe.

What Is Your Worldview?

If you are a Christian and your husband is in the military, you really need to know what he's fighting for: what his cause is. If we are only working to make an income and don't believe in what we are doing (or in what our spouse is doing), then we should really reconsider what field of work we are in. We need to be knowledgeable enough about what our husbands are doing, to be able to answer people when they have questions about our husbands' jobs and what they are doing when deployed. 1 Peter 3:15b-16 says *Always be ready to give a defense to everyone who asks you a reason for the hope that is in you, with meekness and fear; that when they determine you as evildoers, those who revile your good conduct in Christ may be ashamed.* This is important in all that we do in life. But as with everything, the things that you do speak louder than the words that you speak:

Dear Lord, Give me the greatness of heart to see the difference between duty and his love for me. Give me understanding that I may know, when duty calls him he must go. Give me a task to do each day, to fill the time when he's away. And Lord, when he's in a foreign land, keep him safe in your loving hand. And Lord, when duty is in the field, please protect him and be his shield. And Lord, when deployment is so long, please stay with me and keep me strong. Amen. (anon.)

My friend in Tennessee, Stephanie, posted this prayer to her Facebook wall soon after her husband left on his latest deployment. She found this quote on the Internet, but it truly sums up a lot. Her husband spent two deployments in Iraq with my husband, and they became close in a father-and-son bond. Stephanie's post especially broke my heart, because if we had not recently moved to where we are living now, Mike would have been on this deployment with Drew right now. Mike had just returned from his last nine months deployment less than nine months ago, and we are thankful that he is not having to leave,for another nine months. The emotions that these wonderful women go through when their husbands deploy, whether it be for the first or tenth time cannot be captured with mere words.

Challenges of Deployment

Whether this is your first or tenth deployment, it's not something that is simple. I have witnessed strong marriages shaken to the core. I have witnessed marriages broken in two. And at the same time, I have witnessed stable marriages made stronger. Many things that will occur during the deployment cannot be stopped, but some things are avoidable. The enemy would love to take every opportunity to sabotage your marriage. Remember that we have power and we are not to cower in fear. But at the same time, 1 Peter 5:8 says *Be self-controlled and alert. Your enemy the devil prowls around like a roaring lion looking for someone to devour.* John 10:10a says *The thief comes only to steal and kill and destroy.* Realize that the enemy wants to end marriages: any way that he can. In my husband's unit, it is the norm for couples to be on their third marriage. Deployments are tough, but *I* do not want to be the norm.

One thing with which many men struggle is pornography. This is even more prevalent when soldiers are deployed overseas. As a wife, I have witnessed other wives sending their husbands pornographic magazines and encouraging their husbands in this area. As a Christian, this is something that should be avoided to protect your marriage. David, who has been a soldier for over 20 years and is a strong Christian, works primarily with men in a specialized unit:

Pornography is a struggle for many. It's not encouraged in the military, but it is very prevalent. During my first deployment my leader was leaving it around and open for all to see, mainly me, because he knows I'm a Christian. I cut out bathing suits and covered the girls with them. He got really mad, but it was very funny. He didn't do it anymore after that. I could have complained and got him in trouble, but that would have alienated me. Also, pornography is encouraged among peers. It is very hard to deal with, because everyone is lonely and trying to fill the loneliness with porn.

As a Christian

Deployment is something that can easily overtake you if you allow the enemy to do that. Be aware of such schemes. As 1 Peter 5:8 says, *Be alert!* Your marriage will be under even more attack because of the complex combination of separation, lack of communication, and amplified concern. Don't be surprised. We are that light in the world, as overwhelming as that responsibility is, during deployments and times when our husbands are home. We are not expected to be perfect, but we should not blend in with the world in such areas.

We must remember that while it is difficult for us as wives staying behind, it is also difficult for our husbands to be away from us. It's always heartbreaking for David to be away from his family,

It is very hard being away from my family for so long during my deployments. I couldn't imagine doing this without the knowledge that I am doing God's will, whether or not it is difficult or easy. It's like my heart gets ripped out each time I would go. I can understand why couples have such a hard time with deployments. As a protection of your heart, I could see them both hardening themselves to each other in order to make it through. I constantly have to remind myself that it is God's will that I deployed so much. I felt that was what I was called to do. That didn't make it easier not being there as a father and husband. Early on in my marriage I told myself I would never be away from my family like I was. I've learned since not to ever say never. As far as failing, I feel not doing God's will would be failing my family as hard as it will be and has been. I do think maybe I tried too hard to make up time when I was home. I often pushed my family pretty hard to experience what life has to offer. The confidence in knowing I was doing God's will was great, but it was still very hard to be away.

Lola, who is both the spouse of a soldier and is in the military herself, has been left behind while her husband deployed. She has also been deployed:

I think that it is harder being the person staying behind actually! While deployed, although it is isn't easy being away, it is easy to get used to the lifestyle. You can get into a routine and depending on your mindset it really is just you. You don't have to always deal with the stresses of everyday living.

Balance Time and Activities

It is so common to have unavoidable catastrophes occur while the husbands are deployed as I pointed out earlier. At the same time there are also things that can happen during a deployment that with proper planning and foresight could be avoidable. One big mistake that can be made (and it took me several deployments to find the balance in this) is *doing too much*. Yes, you want to keep yourself busy, and it is important that you be productive with your time. It is good to use this time to go to a Bible study, lead a Bible study, learn a new hobby spend time on the ones you already enjoy, take a class, train for a marathon, etc. These are all great things as long as they are in balance. During one deployment I found myself going to a Bible study, leading a youth group of 40 teens, helping start a Hispanic ministry in our church, training for a marathon, taking 3 of the boys to baseball practices and games, preparing 3 of my boys for separate mission trips, and homeschooling all 4 of my sons! It was just *way* too much. It is easy to try to fill the time in a way that is not healthy. *Something will give.* I believe during that time it was my children who suffered, plus I didn't take the time I needed to really focus on my husband's prayer needs and concerns as much as I should have. I didn't really grasp the concept that I was my husband's #1 intercessor at that point.

It would be just as simple to become bored and not know what to do with your free time. This is where it is easy for a lot of women to get into trouble. We all want to do things that make us happy and are enjoyable, and there is nothing wrong with that. It is good to reach out to others who are not Christian and be an example for them and with them. It is another thing to be involved in their activities and dragged down by them. Proverbs 13:20 says *He who walks with the wise grows wise, but a companion of fools suffers harm.* This verse is not saying that you are only to hang out with Christians and just focus on building yourself up all the time, but it is warning you not to become a companion of those who are not living properly. There is a difference between being with someone and reaching out and being a companion to him or her. It is easy to muddle the lines, but as a Christian you need to remember that you are the example.

Make sure that you are involved in your church and going regularly. It's easy to get distracted, get too tired, get too busy, and wind up missing Sunday after Sunday of church. We don't need to be checking off the block by going to church, but we need that fellowship and companionship of other believers. It's also not enough to just go to church and sit in the chair every week, but we need to be involved with other people. It's so easy to isolate ourselves when we are going through a difficult time, but keeping involved with other believers who will pour into our lives and keep us accountable is very important. Always remember that balance is important and not to overextend yourself in commitments and responsibilities. While our husbands are gone, he and our children are our top priorities. It's important to learn to say *no* to people. People who mean well may assume that we have more free time on our hands with our husbands gone. While this can be the case, we also must remember that we are occupying the role of two people while our spouse is gone. So guard your time.

Keep in Constant Contact With Your Husband

During deployment remember that communication with your spouse is key. As much as you are able to, e-mail your husband, send him letters and cards, send him packages regularly, and take the time to listen to him when he needs you. It's frustrating that he is not able to call you much or that you are not able to contact him through the phone whenever you would like to talk to him, but keep in mind how difficult for him it is were he to call you and you were too busy doing something else. Sure you are busy, but often as the wife you may need to stop what you are doing and just listen and speak to your husband. You can always pick the groceries up later or finish the chores you are doing. He generally can't call whenever he wants, and he is limited when he does call.

One complaint that many women have made to me is that when their husbands call, the husbands don't talk much. This is a common occurrence. There are many reasons for this. First of all, he may be so exhausted that he is just too tired to talk. He, also may not be able to share what he is doing, especially if he is on secretive missions. You have to remember that what you are saying on the phone can be heard by others and that we are at war. Try not to grill your husband to get information out of him. He will feel pressured and backed into a wall. Just let him speak when he wants, and really have a listening ear. I have the problem of talking too much when my husband is trying to talk. There is so much I have built up that I want to share, and it is difficult for me to keep my mouth shut. That is another issue that you really need to be prayerful about: how much to share with your husband. I am not talking about lying to your husband,or keeping the truth from him. I'm talking about when he calls and only has a few minutes, he doesn't need all the details of the broken vacuum cleaner and the cat that got stuck on the roof He may be focusing on his mission and doing all he needs to do. It's definitely a fine line.

Your husband will want to know that you are okay and that you are able to cope without him being away, but at the same time,he will want to know that he is needed. Just really tread lightly on how you say things, and listen to the tone of his voice and to what he is saying. If he thinks you completely have it all together and are superwoman with no need of him whatsoever, then he will feel like he is not important or needed. Reassure him that you need him and love him, but also reassure him that you are able to do what you need to do while he is gone. Be sure to resolve issues as they come up, as much as you are able, but don't try to tackle major issues while you are apart.

Send your husband frequent pictures of yourself, the children, and things that your kids may have made or have drawn. Send packages to him with things that he is not able to get on while deployed but enjoys, and have the children be a part of the process. Make sure you make the whole package-sending a fun time for the kids. It's easy to make it like a chore, and the children will catch on to your feelings.

The Deployment Cycles

There is a definite cycle that can be anticipated during a deployment. The first month or two is a time of adjusting to your life without your spouse. This can be and often is a very difficult time. You can become lonely and depressed, and it is easy for fear to set in at this point. This is one reason it is crucial for you to be involved with the body of Christ and active in your church. Get together with some of the other wives whose husbands are gone also. You can be going through similar issues and may be able to help one another along. Often there is comfort in just knowing you are not the only one going through what you are experiencing. During the second part of the deployment cycle, you have probably learned how to cope with your husband being gone and have developed a routine to accomplish all you need to do while he is away. You have probably set up a network for fixing things that need fixing, and this is often a time when we wives get projects done around the house or conquer a goal that we want to accomplish. Always remember to keep things in balance and not over-commit. Also, remember to continue to pray for your husband. As your husband's #1 intercessor, you will need to make sure you spend a lot of time in prayer for him. I would often be awakened at 2:00 or 3:00 a.m. to pray for Mike. Several times I found out that his life was actually in danger during these times. Remember that there is a huge time difference, and the middle of the night for you is daytime for him. Don't view these times of being awakened as insomnia, but realize that they are times for you to pray for your husband.

Remember to allot much time for your children. Allow and encourage them to talk, but realize that it takes time for them to deal with their emotions. If you ask them questions (and that is highly encouraged), they may not reply due to the fact that they haven't gotten a handle of what they are even thinking. Your children will step up to the plate if their dad is gone and if you give them the opportunity. Do not heap on an unreasonable amount of responsibility like expecting your oldest child to babysit the rest of the children for hours every day. Your child is not the parent, and they will become resentful. Encourage them to do more around the house, and praise them when they are doing more. If you just throw everything at them, they will feel like they are taken advantage of, and the deployment will be that much more difficult for them.

Balance, again, is key. The children need to know it is important for them to help more, but at the same time you need to allow them to have a childhood. They can resent their dad if they correlate his being gone or the military in general with their additional chores. With their added responsibility should come more perks. It's not that they are being paid off for helping, but they have earned more rights and freedoms based upon their increased responsibilities.

As the end of the deployment cycle approaches, once again it is easy to get on an emotional roller coaster. You will probably scramble to finish those projects. You may have made new friends while he was gone and have new hobbies and interests. Remember that people change in time, and growth is actually a good thing. As Christians, we need to be growing and improving our character and actions. Just as it is before a deployment, you need to make sure that you clear your schedule as much as you are able to for your husband's return. He needs to know that he is your top priority, and that even though you have spent much time apart he is still the main person in your life. This is an exciting time for the children also. They are anticipating their daddy coming home, and they are anxious and excited!

For very young children and babies, it's vital that you talk about your husband while he is gone ,and show pictures to them. If they do not show excitement that their daddy is coming home, do not pressure them or make them feel bad. Remember that they are just young children, and they are even more confused with their emotions than you are. Clean the house as well as you can, but don't stress out about perfection. Stock-up on groceries and necessities for yourself and your household. You don't want to have to spend time in the grocery store right after your husband gets home, catching up on laundry, or doing errands that you could have done in advance.

Tips from Chapter 10

- If your husband is deployed, remember to not overcommit yourself. Plan more time than you think necessary to accomplish the things you need to do.

• Make a list of your activities and prioritize them. If you are getting stressed out while your husband is deployed, look to see which activities are not necessary while he is gone.

• If you have a friend whose husband is deployed, do what you can to help your friend and not place extra demands on her that would stress her out even more. Put yourself in her shoes and don't judge her for doing anything that you don't think you would do.

Questions from Chapter 10

• What are some things you can do to let your husband know that he's still on your heart and mind while he is gone? Ask your children the same question.

• Do you feel that you have balance in your life? What are some activities and events that you can forgo to make your life less stressful?

• What are some things you can do with your children that would make this time of deployment less difficult for them?

POINTS YOU WANT TO REMEMBER

feel free to jot down notes below...

POINTS YOU WANT TO REMEMBER

feel free to jot down notes below...

- C H A P T E R 1 1 -

Redeployment: I Thought This Was Supposed to Be Like a Honeymoon!

And let us not grow weary while doing good, for in due season we shall reap if we do not lose heart.

Galatians 6:9

Redeployment is the adjustment time following your husband's deployment. This can be the most difficult time of the whole deployment process, especially if we are not aware of the readjustments that will inevitably occur. This should be a time of anticipation and excitement. At the same time while the husband is gone, the wife must take on a form of spiritual authority for her family due to geography. This is a seasonal leadership, and it is often quite difficult to transition back into the allowing our husbands back the authority that he has as the man of the house.

Transition Tips

Here are a few tips to make things run more smoothly when your spouse returns, based on my experience with this redeployment period which I learned most often the hard way)

* Do *not* plan anything major within the first few weeks. This includes parties for him and/or visits to extended relatives. You may think that this is a great time to gather a bunch of people who love him, but in most cases it will be too overwhelming for him. *He* may even think it is a good idea on the phone before he comes home, but you need to realize that he may not be thinking about the time change, the climate change, and all of what he has gone through. It

will take awhile for your husband to process all he has experienced, and throwing him into something like this may be way too much.

*For many men being in a place with a lot of people will be overwhelming. Remember that each husband is different. Just play it by ear and let him dictate what he is comfortable with and what he wants to do. That is one of the reasons that it is so important to keep your schedule open. One thing my husband likes to do when he comes home is to go shopping. My husband is a man of many hobbies: he kayaks, runs, does *Crossfit,* scuba dives, mountain bikes (and the list goes on!). Obviously, while he is deployed he cannot do most of these activities. When he comes home, he not only wants to do these hobbies but he wants to *get* stuff for them. I find it amusing to see so many soldiers milling around Walmart and other large stores right after their deployments, but I can understand the need to see the newest items and what they have missed while they were gone.

*If you have small children or babies, don't expect him to jump right back in and be able to babysit. I have a friend whose husband came home from being deployed, and she went to the grocery store for a short while and came home. When she came back, her husband was sitting on the floor crying, and the children were just staring at him. Her husband is a wonderful man and was always very active in his children's lives, so it really came as a huge surprise. Realize that your husband has not been dealing with children for a long time, and that his mission while deployed was something altogether different. Do not make him feel stupid or incompetent by making a big deal about it if something like this occurs.

*Do not expect the children to be able to jump in where they left off. They may be uncomfortable and need some time to reacquaint. Especially if they are younger, it is common for the children to cry and feel uncomfortable. Tell your husband that this is a possibility in advance and that he doesn't need to take it personally. He probably still will, so be prepared to be an encouragement and comfort to both your children and to your husband. Sometimes the children are angry that their dad was gone, because they just can't grasp what is going on like we as adults can. It is up to you as the wife to be the mediator and to make things run as smoothly as you are able to. Your reactions to the behavior of the children or the sadness of your husband will often determine how long something like this will be drawn out.

*Make sure you give yourself as a couple time to reacquaint. You have to remember that you haven't seen each other for a long time, and you both have changed and gone through things that may need time to work through. Don't expect him to jump into your schedule, but make him and his getting readjusted your #1 goal. He may have been through a lot of things that you don't know about, and it may take time for him to be able to share this with you. Remember that there is also a time change, and it may take awhile for your husband to get back on schedule. Keep in mind that every person is different also. Some men may want to talk about what they have gone through immediately, and for some it may take a long time for them to be able to get out what they have been through. Try not to shut him down when he does talk by cutting him off and saying that it is too much for you to hear. He may have gone through quite a bit, and he needs you there to listen to him.

*Watch your words and your tone. If the things he tells you are too detailed for you, gently ask him to avoid some of the details if at all possible. The way you react to what he says and does can either shut him down or help him to deal with what he's been through. Proverbs 15:1 says *A gentle answer turns away wrath, but a harsh word stirs up anger.* That is such a key verse in any relationship. How you react to what is said makes such a difference in whether or not something insignificant can turn into a huge argument. Always be gentle in your tone and in your attitude. Yes, it might go completely against your emotions, but remember what a benefit it will be to your communication!

Remember that redeployment is a process and not just a momentary event. Your husband may have been gone for a long time, so it will probably take a while for things to get back to normal in your household. Where you have been the one to make all the decisions, do all the disciplining of the children, and taking care of everyday concerns, it's important that you reintegrate your husband back into *your* life. That sounds so cold, but you have to remember that it will take time. Don't thrust all the responsibilities back at him before he has had time to adjust, but slowly as he is ready let him take the reigns back as the man of the house. He will not do everything perfectly, but as always encourage him and build him up.

Keep Things as Positive as Possible

Keep in mind that your husband's deployment was a *positive* thing. He is a hero who has made a huge difference in this world. Sure, it was a huge sacrifice for your entire family, but you made it through, and hopefully grew because of it. Remember that you are a missionary family, and he just got back from a huge mission trip. It's exciting to know that your husband was able to make an impact for the kingdom of God. Psalm 2:8 says *Ask of me, and I will make the nations your inheritance, the ends of the earth your possession.* Your family has impacted the nations (literally), and you can have confidence in that. The following is a great article on what many soldiers experience both during and after they are being reintegrated back into their families. These are things that most people do not talk about, and those who have not gone through deployments could not even imagine. I know that my husband gets antsy for adventure often. If he is not busy doing activities and keeping preoccupied, this could easily be the case with him:

Married to a Veteran

When Memories of Past Interrupt the Present

E. C. Hurley, Ph.D. {Ret. Army Col.)

Every day I see veterans in my office who are battling to recover their lives after honorably serving our county. Resuming life after war is not easy. Some will take a few weeks to adjust to life 'back in the world' as they cope with new family responsibilities and performance demands at the military installation. Other veterans, with unresolved combat trauma, demonstrate greater adjustment difficulties. Their relationship survived the difficulties of military deployments but new difficulties emerge that threaten to jeopardize their future now that they are together again.

Everyone returns changed from a combat deployment. Spouses of combat soldiers frequently report their partner is typically less communicative, more emotionally distant, socially isolated, irritable, and more reactive. They generally report that the honeymoon period after coming home may have lasted three days, perhaps even a couple of weeks before the difficulties began. Many soldiers who have experienced multiple deployments often express they would be more comfortable being back down range living in the combat zone since it is easier than being home where everything takes so much effort.

When the news announced that Operation Iraqi Freedom (OIF) was over, many veterans had difficulty accepting the announcement -- it was not over for them. For these veterans, it seems there is no safe place anymore. They continue to struggle to make sense of it all. In many ways, one or more tours of duty have redefined their lives. It is difficult to transition from a deployment in which every day other peoples' lives depended on them to returning home to a regular routine without a sense of wartime urgency and 'mission.' For many veterans who have served honorably, the past continues to influence, if not control, their lives. It is as if the veteran is still fighting the war. Spouses report that sometimes they feel like the enemy. Many veterans report they have lost the ability to turn loose of an argument.

Emotional reactivity is common among many veterans. Such response is known as 'being triggered.' Something in the present situation sets them off and they tend to react without thinking. Add to the situation that the spouse may have their own unresolved memories of past events. For example, if a spouse grew up with abandonment issues as a child, the veteran's emotional numbness and withdrawal can trigger an emotional reaction for both persons. The couple *begins to react to each other in a manner which seems out of control. It is like they are in a dance in which no one is leading. One wife told me, 'he has been back four months; I have been waiting for him to tell me that he loves me. I finally asked **Do you love me?** He stated, **I don't care about anything.'***

It's hard to imagine a wife not taking this personally. But in reality, the veteran's statement was not about his love for his wife, it was about emotional numbness due to living in an environment where you might die at any moment. Thinking about how much you love someone in that life-threatening environment can create depression, generate more anxiety, and eventually can get you killed. It is easier to numb out. He perceived his spouse as becoming argumentative. He later stated, 'I thought my job was to get as many rounds down range as possible' during the argument. There are some events in our lives in which unresolved memories continue to impact our present lives. For veterans, this means that some rules of engagement as well as intense combat experiences can be triggered and relived as if they are happening in the present.

Brian voices what soldiers frequently feel. For many soldiers it's not only the experiences that occur when they are deployed that are difficult, but the returning process can be quite frustrating also:

Deployments were great because I was busy all the time. Sometimes I was doing other people's work but I didn't care, because I love to work and learn. As far as experiences go, I had a lot of good experiences and a few bad ones, but overall all my deployments went well. Returning home as a single soldier was difficult for me because I like to be around my buddies, and when we came home everyone went their separate ways for leave (vacation) and I would end up back home with my parents. Not that I don't love them, but I just didn't want to be asked a million questions after coming home to people that couldn't understand what I went through.

There have been many suicides and homicides in the military community, and many of these are within the special operational soldiers and their families. My husband's theory is that it is not necessarily due to PTSD but to the fact that most of these types of units deploy so frequently and with not much time in between to allow time for them to be a normal family again. I know that for the 11 years that we lived in Clarksville, we lived that lifestyle: Mike would be gone on deployment, and when he would come home they would jump right into training for the next deployment. That is not an exaggeration but a reality. Mike has said this is taking a toll on the families, and these massive suicides and homicides are proof of that. He said these guys just snap due to the crazy amount of pressure that is on them. They are constantly on *performance* mode, and there is no downtime for them.

I often had to put myself in coping mode just to get by. I found it necessary to compartmentalize my feelings and emotions, which, if I had left them non-segmented, could be quite toxic to my marriage. Coping is often viewed by onlookers as strength, but it is more akin to putting up walls to block off your emotions so that you can do the things that needs to be done in a way that won't cause you to break down. As I write this now, the tears flow thinking back on all the pains that we endured. I think that now that I am not living in that situation, I can finally let my defenses down and allow myself to acknowledge these feelings..

For the soldiers, they also have to set up barriers and walls in their emotions to accomplish the things that they do overseas. For some, their job while deployed is something completely different than while they are in the States. They must be on mission mode so that they can jump from task to task quickly and efficiently. Their lives are at stake as are the lives of others. They must rapidly make decisions which can differ in each occasion, based on the situation they are in. If they are dealing with the local soldiers and the local people, they must know who to trust and who not to trust. And often it's intuitive. This can change based on whether the locals change in who they *decide* they will see as the bad guys for that day. It's often based on money. Mike has met some very wonderful local soldiers, interpreters, etc. who he has loved tremendously while he was in the Middle East. But he was completely aware that the culture is vastly different than our western culture. His way of thinking had to shift based upon how he knows the people there would think and respond.

For many soldiers, going from that type of mentality and mindset with a heightened sense of anticipation, (and borderline paranoia) back into the *normal* world of family life with crying babies, fast food, and the rest of life in America, this change is often overwhelming. If you are a wife whose husband has returned and it seems like he is still wearing his *battle armor,* try to gently help him to take his armor off and return to an unhardened state. It is also very important to realize that this will take time, prayer, and a gentle disposition as a wife.

Unfortunate Tragedy

I am including this story that many have already heard about, but I am wanting to point out the magnitude of the effect on the children, and how completely incomprehensible to many this life of the military family can sometimes be. There have been a few bouts of killing frenzies when soldiers have returned home from deployment. Most of these are in the specialized units. The first spree was dubbed by the media as *Ft. Bragg / Fayetteville's Bloody Summer* as there were many incidents in a short period of time. Within a six-week period, four wives were killed, then the husbands committed suicide. I read a book by a great reporter who chronicled the events of each of these tragic events. My information is not from that source. I have questioned a friend of mine, Geraldine, who not only knew one of the couples who both tragically lost their lives but who also wound up having guardianship of their three sons throughout the ordeal. To protect the privacy of the sons and their parents' actions, I am going to just completely omit their names and location.

The husband came back from a deployment, and his wife wanted a divorce. This was something she had planned and something that took him by surprise. He killed her in a fit of rage and buried her body in a panic, making it look like she was missing. This is where Geraldine comes in. She was asked by the husband to watch the boys while he looked for his missing wife. Her body was found and he went to jail. Geraldine did what she could to be a good care-giver to these boys, including doing boy activities with them. She took them to the jail to see their dad along with a male pastor at the church. She took care of them until they were able to get to their relative's house. It was after they left that their dad wound up hanging himself in the jail. It's all so sad and tragic, and, of course, there will always be questions that are unanswered.

I asked Geraldine if she felt that there would be anything that could have been done differently to help the family in the first place: perhaps, something that could have prevented the incident from getting as bad as it got...

All in all people CANNOT stop an action like the husband's in their homes, behind closed doors. I do think the military could have done a better job of supporting separated families. If anything, just support groups and NOT being faced with discipline if a family member comes forth and has problems. I also (my opinion) think that families should NOT have such long tours.

Helping this family was a very sacrificial thing for my friend Geraldine to do, and it was extremely heart wrenching for her to have to see these young boys going through such a mind-boggling ordeal:

You are simply never prepared for something like this. God must have gotten me through this, because those children were safe and loved until their family got there.

I would like to point out that Geraldine's family is not military. This has not prevented her from helping a family that is. She and her family were literally being Jesus' hands and feet to a family that was severely hurting. She helped to provide comfort and whatever form of peace she could for some young boys that were in complete turmoil. I believe that she is a definite example for many.

PTSD and Redeployment

PTSD (Post-traumatic Stress Disorder) is a word that is often associated with military coming back from deployments. There is much research that is still being made on the subject, and the military is trying to do what they can to help their soldiers. But there are still may problems with the kinds of help that is available. My friend, Malachias, who is a combat veteran who suffers from PTSD has spent years trying to get help via the military system:

The problem is two-fold. We are teaching everyone to be co-dependent. As a Soldier with PTSD, we are pushed to be dependent on medications, therapy, support groups etc... But when these are finally seen as simply a mask to the situation, we become isolated because 'nothing' that's supposed to work or help us works. But we are pushed to seek counseling, take your meds and whatnot. We never get to the core of the problem.

I was just having a conversation today about this similar situation with a fellow Soldier at work. We no longer take the time to invest into each other what the person needs. Most people are investing into them what they want them to be.

When it comes to the churches role, here is my problem. People constantly say 'I'm praying for you.' How about take the time to actually pray with them. It has become a designated and default response to someone who is having a problem. Words have power, but they have exponential power when we back them up with action! We need to stop teaching dependence. It happens in our public schools and in every institution we are a part of. How about we teach proper mentoring, how to be an individual and work on your problems without avoiding them. We need to teach people to be problem solvers within the realm of who they are. You cannot successfully be part of a greater community or group or whatever if you have no clue how to take care of yourself first. Only then can you and are you able to help others.

Tips from Chapter 11

- If you know of a family whose husband is coming home from deployment, think of ways that you could help to make this transition time easier for them: make meals, offer to babysit when they are ready, offer to watch their home if they go on vacation, etc.

• If your husband is getting ready to come home from a deployment, give him time to readjust. Don't throw every responsibility back onto him immediately, but give him time to reintegrate. Be patient with him, as his job overseas is completely different than at home.

• Don't be frustrated and bitter by unmet expectations. Be patient and allow enough time to transition.

Questions from Chapter 11

• What are some things you can do to help your husband transition more easily when he comes home from being deployed?

• Are you expecting him to come back completely unchanged, or are you aware that people change with time and circumstance? Are you praying for this transition time?

• Are you preparing your children for their dad's return? Are you helping them to transition also, as they won't automatically understand that this is necessary?

POINTS YOU WANT TO REMEMBER

feel free to jot down notes below...

Nicole Brocx Lee

POINTS YOU WANT TO REMEMBER
feel free to jot down notes below...

- CHAPTER 12 -

Deployments Affect Marriages

Nevertheless let each one of you in particular so love his own wife as himself, and let the wife see that she respects her husband.

Ephesians 5:33

In the military community it seems almost commonplace to speak of deployments. The affects of such a huge event on a family's life is not even comprehensible to those who have not had to endure such episodes, and often repeatedly.

Affairs

Affairs are sadly a common occurrence in the military community. With the spouse so often gone, either on deployments or trainings, wives are left home alone. There is a loneliness and sometimes desperation that can creep in if unguarded.

We all know stories of the young wife whose husband leaves for training and she finds a guy and has an affair. We wonder *How could she do this to him? He's fighting for, training for or defending our country and freedom. How selfish of this woman! Just as soon as her husband is out the front door, her roving eyes are looking for a man to fill his place. Does she have no respect? What if you found out that woman was a good friend of yours? Would you reconsider how you thought of her?*

Well, that woman was me. No, I wasn't out searching for a man the minute my husband walked out the door to go overseas. Yes, I was a young, immature and lonely wife. I wasn't bored, I worked and had friends to keep myself busy. But I wasn't being careful with the time I was spending with this person, mainly because I didn't have a clue that I was setting myself up for failure. We weren't in a church at the time, so I had no spiritual guidance or knowledge of what was or was not appropriate. These are not excuses for my behavior and betrayal, but looking back and also looking on other couples that stumble I can see where they can easily slip through the cracks on their marriage.

It's also great that everything we go through can be a learning experience if we allow it. I've definitely not been perfect in any way, shape, or form throughout the marriage, and I have had unfortunate repeat performances of some mistakes. But I know that God has been with me every step of the way and has spoken to me to prevent me from making even more dire mistakes than I have made. I am thankful for a husband who has been caring, loving, and gracious.

God always finds place for redemption and grace, even in and after our mistakes. The amazing ending to this story is that Mike actually ran into the guy I had the affair with at the beginning of our marriage, many years later, in another country on deployment! Mike was able to verbally offer him forgiveness and put an end to the guilt that had been hanging on this man's shoulders for over 20 years. This experience and many other ones allow me to know how to help younger military women to be able to know how to be on guard and combat their hearts from what the enemy will throw their way. It's always easier for one to take advice from someone who has been through the same things that they have been or are contemplating rather than someone just offering them advice with no personal knowledge of the issues at hand.

It's so important that we older women stand beside these younger women who are having struggles in many ways. Titus 2:3-5 tells us how we should be helping the younger women: *The older women likewise, that they be reverent in behavior, not slanderers, not given to much wine, teachers of good things – that they admonish the young women to love their husbands, to love their children, to be discrete, chaste, homemakers, good, obedient to their own husbands, that the word of God may not be blasphemed.* That's a lot to swallow, but the first step is knowing our role as older women in helping these younger women and not to assume that they have it all together. To the outside I probably looked like I was strong and had it going on, but we all struggle inside and we all need one another.

I look back on Mike's whole military time and think of ways that I could have been helped, encouraged and taught. I don't think of this to wonder why I didn't get the help I needed (as I often didn't think I needed help), but this helps me to better open my eyes to the needs of those around me. *Younger* doesn't merely refer to age, but it can be anyone who is struggling with something we have already experienced and have the ability to help them.

Allowing Our Husbands to Lead the Family

There is a great song that really exemplifies all that it means for a husband to be a leader of the home. This, of course, is not just for military families but for all families. Listen to it if you get the chance *(Lead Me* by Sanctus Real). For many men, it's easy to get wrapped up in their jobs and make their careers a priority over their families. For military soldiers it can often become their identities, and I have witnessed countless marriages go downhill because the husband has worshipped his career and placed his being a soldier over his being a husband and father.

As wives, we want our husbands to lead our families. But at the same time, we often don't allow our husbands to be the leaders God has called them to be. We want someone to lead and take charge, but at the same time we often want the control. This is one area where the older women (or the ones who have gone through this) can help the younger women to find balance and harmony in their marriages. We don't need to become our husband's shadows, but at the same time we do need to be a support to them in all things.

Allowing our husbands to lead our families is not something that comes naturally. But in doing so,we are showing our husbands the respect that they need so that they have the confidence to be that leader that we all long for our husbands to be.

Divorce

As common as divorce is in the civilian world (above 50%), the rate of divorce among the military community is considerably higher. We have just moved from a town (not a small town) that is right in the middle of the Bible belt, and the divorce rate in that town is 89 percent! I find that to be appalling. If there are churches on almost every corner of the street,and Christians are supposedly everywhere, then what is the reason for such a high rate of divorce?

Marriage is supposed to mirror the relationship between Jesus and the church. As a Christian in the military, your marriage is on display for those who are looking for hope. The enemy's goal is to steal, kill, and destroy. One of the ways that he does this best is by ruining our marriages. We realize the additional demands that this lifestyle puts on our marriage. If our husbands deploy, we know that these demands are even more magnified.

One of the most devastating things that can happen to a family is divorce. It's the collapse of relationships, dreams, and security. Not only are the husband and wife harmed, but the children are also deeply affected. So many times, deployments cause communication to crumble which puts a huge strain on marriages. It's difficult enough as a *single* mom trying to fulfill that role of the mother and the father while the husband is gone, but also add to that the lack of communication (willing or not) due to circumstances and can be devastating to a marriage. I have seen many marriages in the military fall apart. Upon reading these surveys that I sent out, I see that several of these women have sought help from the church for marriage problems that they have had. It's not a surprise when a person's marriage is suffering, and often they just need someone more mature to come beside them and give them some spiritual counsel and encouragement to help them out. I myself have gotten so frustrated at how this seemingly simple aspect is lacking in most churches.

Lola is not only a military wife, but she is also in the Army and has been in for six years. She understands that it's not easy to be in the military as a Christian:

You could say it is difficult being a Christian in the military, but it all really depends on how you react to your surroundings. Most of the time you aren't surrounded by a bunch of God-loving people, and with a demanding job and such a diverse Army you always have to be aware of your attitude. Actions speak louder than words and living that is the most important part of being Christian no matter what your occupation is. The main challenge is the diversity and maintaining your Christianity. To help overcome those challenges it helps to stay in the Word and in constant prayer.

Lola has insight into the demands that the military has on a Christian soldier, so it also helps her to better pray for her husband.

One of the most important things we can do for both our husbands and our marriages is to pray for them daily. We have more insight into our husband's needs than anyone else. We are his intercessor. An intercessor is a negotiator who acts as a link between parties. As a Christian intercessor for our husbands, when you pray for him you are his mediator who is praying on his behalf. We need not only to be praying for protection and provision but also that our husbands would be the Christian men that God has called Him them to be. Our husbands may or may not be covered in prayer by prayer-chains or Bible study groups (which is great), but it's even more important that we personally pray for them. Not only will this help him spiritually, but it will also open our eyes to what his needs are.

We often forget that prayer is not just making our requests known to God, but we are also to listen to Him and our hearts and minds will be more conformed to His will. We don't change God's mind the more that we pray, but we learn more about what He wants of us and what is best for us. Surprisingly, we often don't know what's best for us. Looking back, we can all be thankful that we are not in control of our lives: God is. We would surely mess up our lives if we were the only contributing factor in determining our outcome.

Sarah is a single mom with two daughters and has recently gone through a divorce with a military soldier:

Yes, I did go to church. I don't attend the same church because across the board I saw too many people getting hurt. This particular church did not at all know how to deal with military families going through divorce. I personally felt judged because of my divorce. I went to another church and felt the same exact way. I just quit going to church for a while, because I was so upset that no one understood my struggle. I felt like I was supposed to just be over the divorce. I tried to deal with it on my own. I don't feel like churches are equipped to deal with family crises when it comes to military. Some of what a military spouse goes through can be conflicting with the word of God. The church needs to be chasing these lost souls that are going into a battle zone that has more demonic activity than we Americans can imagine. Man, if the church would pour into the military families like the Word says, you would see the divorce rate go down.

Abuse

Sadly abuse can be a common occurrence, and I have known many women who are living in a lifestyle of abuse with seemingly no way out. I was in an abusive relationship when I was a teenager, so I know how something that doesn't start out dark and ugly can turn into a trap in which you feel there is no hope. In a Christian marriage this is even more confusing, especially when women don't feel like they can share these things with others.

Gabby and Daniel both grew up in Christian homes, and he was a missionary to other countries before they decided together to go into the military with the specific intent of being a light in a dark place. The following is part of their story. As I have seen, so many marriages struggle and waver. I think that their story will help people to better understand the stresses that a military lifestyle can cause on a marriage.

I met Daniel in church, and he was a missionary serving in YWAM (Youth With a Mission). We fell in love and had similar life goals. We wanted to marry, but he wanted a stable job that would provide for us. He knew I admired people who served in the military, so he said in slight frustration 'I should just join the Air Force.' I agreed, excitedly. Of course, we prayed about this decision but decided that it would become a new mission field for us. We knew that the career field was dark and paved with many divorces, broken marriages, affairs, and immorality, but we really believed that God was calling us to be like Daniel in the Bible and stand for what was right by being salt and light in the darkness.

Then Daniel was introduced to all of the temptations involved. I was aware of it. We were aware of it. We knew it would be hard but did not understand how much of a temptation Daniel would have to overcome before he would truly be a light. Little did we know how much his faith would be tested: if it really was his faith or his parents' faith that he was living.

After Daniel and Gabby had been married for four years, knowing the struggles Gabby was going through in her marriage, I asked if she was involved in any support group within her husband's unit. She initially started going after they had moved overseas. But then Gabby got a job, and her time was more limited.

Most of the wives have small children and meet during the day or have meetings during the base youth group that I volunteer for. By going to the meetings, I have met a core group of women who I connected with and can share my concerns about everything going on in my life. They are willing to help as much as they can. These women have helped me through the hard TDY's and concerns I had about communication throughout. The rest of the wives I do not relate to or connect with, and it seems like forced friendships based on the mere fact that our husbands share the same job. We have a key spouse who checks in on us monthly, but unfortunately she knows less about the military than I do and I feel as if she has a harder time coping with her husband's job than I do.

When we first moved overseas, I was really excited about finding a church to attend. Daniel lost interest in attending church, and we shared a car. Sometimes he would not make it home from the night before due to being out with the guys. Since we lived close enough to base to walk, I walked to church. I decided that, although it is the chapel, I liked that it was close to me, and the people who I saw on Sunday were people who I would see throughout the week and maintain a relationship with. Most of the churches off base were far away, and cultural differences made it harder to mesh with the transient lifestyle we live. Now, the chapel is home to me. The messages are not as deep as I would like them to be all the time and it is harder to see God moving, but I understand that this is a season in my life and the friendships I have formed are monumental and uplifting, causing me to desire the spiritual maturity that I see displayed in others lives.

I will never forget describing my unhappy marriage to a woman in the church who I trusted. She flat out asked me if I knew about abusive relationships. It was empowering having someone ask and be so correct with the behavior. It was as if someone showed me how much better a light bulb was than a candle. Instead of telling me to pray for my husband, cook, clean, have more sex, and be a better wife, someone put the burden on him and said that he had a major role in the dysfunction of our marriage. She pointed me towards books written by Christian women on the subject of abuse. It gave me the correct tools to navigate a relationship with someone who was controlling and manipulative. It was eerie at times reading the books because I saw my relationship written in the pages; no marriage book I had read could pinpoint the behaviors I saw in my husband. The authors also pointed out that I was also at fault for letting myself be treated that way. I could get out, but it would require strength. Standing up for myself was hard at first because my pride told me that I was not emotional and being cursed at and devalued daily should not hurt because I got my worth from God. Oh, the lies we tell ourselves to save a relationship.

Once I got past that and started standing up to him and going to his authorities he no longer had power to treat me any way he pleased. One reason I delayed in standing up to him and calling him on his bluffs was because I knew it would mean termination of our relationship. The first time I called his First Shirt and told him that my husband was threatening me with divorce all the time was the final straw that caused Daniel to start to file the ERD that would send me home. His supervisor had a meeting with him and told him to make his intentions clear to me. My husband called after the meeting and wanted to know why I was being so mean about the whole issue. He told me he had wanted a divorce for 2 1/2 years straight before I involved his work. The only way I could risk ending my relationship with my husband by standing up for myself was because God placed beautiful people in my life who supported me. They never pressured me into reporting his abusiveness, but provided validation and always told me that I deserved better and did not deserve the abuse. Just having them listen and confirm my sanity and say that I had reasonable expectations of Daniel was more helpful than they will ever know... like calling while he was TDY for example.

Abuse is taboo in the church. Most women believe the unwritten rule that if your husband is not having an affair, then the marriage is to be saved even at the cost of yourself as a person. I never realized that my husband's abusiveness made me shut down parts of my personality and creativity. The reason I forced myself to become less emotional was so he could not hurt me. Shutting off emotions is shutting off a reflection of God in your life. By doing this, I put my dreams on hold for someone who should have been helping me realize them. This was never what God intended and I am glad that by His grace I am set free. It's hard moving on and I miss the man I fell in love with, but I know that person will only exist again if God rescues Daniel. I still pray for this day to come because my husband was once a wonderful and loving person, but that person has been replaced by someone who is hardened and totally dishonest. It's shocking to see the stark contrast. Without God someone's personality can totally change. Scary.

Sadly, Gabby was trying to cling on to a marriage where she was the only party wanting the marriage to last. We cannot make someone else change his or her mind. We can try to point things out, but ultimately every person is responsible for his or her own choices. Do you remember Tristen in Chapter 3 who told us how much she loved traveling in the military? She tells us about her own divorce that happened later:

Two years ago I said I loved military life, but my life

145

ended up breaking me. I was left with four kids (two with autism), no support, no help, and no end in sight. When my husband left for a 6-12 month deployment, I thought I would make it. I didn't. The strain of daily life with no help was too much for me. I felt overwhelmed, unloved, and forgotten. I was a 27-hour drive from my own family, and trying to attend school while trying to deal with the special needs and circumstances of my family. I came very close to suicide. I had asked the grandmother of my stepchildren to take them for two weeks, because I just needed a break. When it didn't happen, it seemed like my whole world caved in around me. I told my husband that I would be leaving when he returned. He came home on emergency leave, and I moved out the same day. It's amazing how much things can change in four months.

Before my marriage I thought I could handle anything that came my way. I know now that I am not a super hero... I think everyone else knows that now, also. When I asked for help, when I told people I wasn't doing well, when I told them I couldn't handle it, they ignored me. I begged for help, and no one would listen. They only offered encouragement and told me that I was doing a great job. I didn't need words of wisdom:I needed actual help. The military was all too happy to send my husband away and pay for my anti-depressants and therapy, but there was no real help.

Now, I genuinely feel happiness: happiness that I hadn't experienced in a very long time. I have support in my life. I am engaged to be married, I'm three days away from my college graduation, and I have a job waiting for me in my field. I now know what it feels like to have a happy family, to enjoy waking up everyday, and to be loved.

It really takes both sides to make a marriage work. But it only takes one person to decide not to try, and the marriage is over.

A Soldier's Perspective

For Brian, his military life has changed drastically from the time he was a single soldier and not living his life for the Lord to being married with baby number two on the way. When we are married, we have more people to think about than just ourselves and our career. As a Christian, our family is on top of the priority ladder above career:

Being married and having children is without a doubt the best thing that has happened to me in my life. It has definitely forced me to settle down. My wife and daughter have completely changed the way I look at my job. Before I would volunteer for everything and try and stay as busy as possible, but now I finish my work and head home to spend as much quality time with my family as possible. Being married has also refocused my thoughts on my career. I have made some changes to my plans for the Army, and I don't feel the need to try and do everything myself. I have learned to let others do their work so I can do mine and go home to my family. I didn't choose to come to the job that I'm now working. But since I do not deploy while here, I realize that once I got settled in , it's been a great time to reconnect with my wife and watch my daughter grow.

David is another Christian soldier. Like Daniel, he also faces the difficulties of being in the military. But he has remained strong in his faith in spite of all that goes on around him. He is not the norm when it comes to being a military soldier, and his life reflects the words that he says. When I asked him what it was like to be a Christian in the military, he had this to share:

Military Regulation states that you cannot proselytize, preach or try to convert people. I don't see it as a limitation because our lives reflect who we are, and if we are Christians, our lifestyle and true love should speak louder than words. We should preach the Gospel through our actions, even our mess-ups and failures. But I have been able to share a lot. What I have found is that being an example is the best way to share my faith. Sometimes, I'm asked about my belief. During counseling, I will hold Christians to a higher standard (as long as I feel they are strong in their beliefs). To weaker Christians, I will often throw in some Biblical truths here and there. Often Christians are made fun of for their beliefs. I see that as an opportunity to share. They are opening the door for me being able to share the love of Jesus, so I take advantage of it and talk as much as I have the opportunity to. I don't get messed with much, but I do see and know Christians are really messed with for their faith. I have been messed with a little, but again, to me that is an invitation to share or get the information and share later, one on one.

Tips from Chapter 12

• Whether or not you're military, think of some battles you've gone through in life and ways that you can use your experiences to help those *younger* than you. Do not judge those whose struggles are not your own.

• Start a small group of younger women/wives who you can help. Do a book study with them on something that would pertain to them, and be open and ready to share your experiences with them.

• Pray for the military families and marriages that appear to be struggling and for those that show no signs of struggles. Start a prayer group for military families to cover them in prayer.

Questions from Chapter 12

• Do you know any military couples who need help in any form? If you can't help them personally, can you point them in the direction of where they can find help: your church, a small group, another military couple that you know would be willing to offer them direction?

• What are some groups in your city that are reaching out to military families? What are they doing for them during deployments? Can you get involved in something like this?

• If you are a military spouse, what are some areas that you see lacking in your marriage? What can you do to improve in those areas? Do you have an older woman with whom you feel comfortable sharing your struggles ?

POINTS YOU WANT TO REMEMBER

feel free to jot down notes around the margins...

- CHAPTER 13 -

What Happened to the Kids?

Behold, children are a heritage from the Lord, the fruit of the womb is a reward. Like arrows in the hands of a warrior, so are the children of one's youth. Happy is the man who has a quiver full of them; they shall not be ashamed, but shall speak with their enemies in the gate.

Psalm 127:3-5

Just writing the heading of this chapter brings tears to my eyes. I hadn't even planned on writing an entire chapter on this topic, but after I wrote a survey for military wives I decided I should get the viewpoints of some of the kids who were raised in homes where their fathers deployed. Because 9/11 occurred over 11 years ago, most of the children who I interviewed are now in their early to late-20's. I did not realize the emotion that would come up with the answers that were written, both from those writing the stories and myself.

Even though my husband was gone often for trainings and school, what I believe really affected my sons the most in my own family were the times when my husband started deploying overseas. Soon after we moved to Tennessee, the deployments began. It's very difficult on children to move, start in a new home, get new friends. Add that to the fact that their dad is gone more than he is home and that his life is in danger when he's gone, and that's almost too much for most children to handle. My husband was and is a great father, and he spends almost all of the time that he is at home with us. He has poured into our four sons' lives like no man I have

149

ever seen, and I do believe that this is one of the reasons that they are able to be the strong and independent men that they are today. Having said that,, it doesn't mean that this season of their lives was not extremely difficult for them.

Several months ago I found a journal that my oldest, Keir, had started the day that 9/11 happened. Reading through it made me laugh and also cry. Because I home-schooled them and had a dentist appointment that morning for a root canal, Keir was able to watch the news for several hours on the day of the tragedy. Now that he is 27, looking back on how he reacted and viewed things at 15 is pretty interesting:

Growing up, my family was a little superstitious when it came to words. I thought that anything you said would cause ripples in the world that could either create or destroy. To say that I hated somebody was the worst thing in the world, and I could never take it back. Anyways, one day my dad and I had a fight. He had recently come back from Iraq and didn't know how to relate to the sons he missed out on growing up. We were young men, but he still saw us as little boys. For me it was especially hard because I had stepped in as the man of the house while he was gone.

I don't remember what the fight was about exactly, but I distinctly remember going into my room, sitting on my bed, and saying 'I hate you, Daddy.' He never heard me say it, but I did. I said the forbidden words.

I wish that I never said that. They were only small words of anger by a teenage boy... but if I could erase that moment, I would. It's the only thing I have ever regretted saying

Reading through these stories from others in military families has really helped me to reconnect with many that I hadn't had heart-to-heart conversations with for awhile (and for some never before). So many were willing to open up and share their concerns and stories. Many had even expressed to me how this was the first time they had ever been able to sit down and process the things that had gone on in their lives. For many, this has been a time of healing by just being able to reminisce and process all that they had to go through. I am thankful that I was able to play some small part in this area of their lives, and I want to take this moment to thank all of you who have shared your stories with me for the benefit of others.

Elisabeth's Story

Elisabeth is 15 years old and lives in North Carolina. Her family is one of the first families that I met in North Carolina, and I fell in love with every member of their family. She had a lot to share that I really feel shows the life of a military child. Elisabeth's candid responses to the questions asked of her are really enlightening:

My dad was deployed most of my younger years. He would leave for about 40 days every 3 months, and even when he was home, he would leave before we got up and get home just 1-2 hours before we went to bed, so I very rarely got to have interaction with him. A few years ago, he had a 12-month deployment to Qatar, which was his major deployment that I could remember. This was his last deployment, for, to put it in exactly his words he's 'throwing in his retirement papers as soon as he can fill them out.' He's scheduled to be on terminal leave starting in November of 2012. Terminal leave is time that a military term meaning the time a person takes off before they retire.

Not having a father-figure there for me during my childhood was a little difficult, I would suppose, but I never knew it any other way. My three siblings, Gregory, Charles, Anne, and I, had to step up and help my mom out when he was gone. We all knew, even at the young ages we were, that it was difficult for her to be with us without him helping.

I think that lots of good things have come from being in a military family. I think the good part that came from it was that I learned to grow up, very fast. With my dad being gone and my parent's divorce in the middle of it all, I had to be mature. Some people might see it as a bad thing that I never got to have a full childhood, but I think it's helpful. It really helped me get along with people, because I acted so much older than I was, especially when I left homeschooling and went to private school. It definitely helped with my communication with adults, because even at 9 years old, I wasn't acting like a 9-year-old, so I could talk to them and have mature conversations. Having friends that I gained through my father being in the Army that wound up moving away assisted with me learning to let go and move on, and also how to stay in contact even through distance. Other positive things about being in the military include being able to go to military functions, having military benefits, and getting to talk to officials, so I further understood the Army and our government. As much as I hate being tied to the military, it has definitely helped me develop and be enlightened of the world around me, I wouldn't have wanted anything different.

I was part of a church while my dad was deployed, and yes, they could have done a lot more to help. Since I was living with my mom at the time, they didn't know much about my dad's deployment. They knew it was happening, but since my father and my mother were far from getting along at the time, they just ignored it. They never, not once in the year that he was gone, talked to me about it or asked me if I was okay or any other gesture of courtesy. There were a lot of times where I missed my dad, so much, that it was painful for me. I know that some of them saw this pain, but they never did anything for me. It almost felt like I was invisible. What I really wanted was for someone to check up on me, and act like they cared, regardless of sincerity.

In many of the surveys I have found that several, if not most of the now young adults, felt overlooked while their fathers were deployed. As church we really need to reach out to those that are hurting. Often we don't know who the hurting are, but just given the circumstances, we can understand that children whose fathers are deployed really need that extra concern shown to them and attention for which they most often will not verbally ask. Dylan, now a 15-year old says,

I feel as if the church could've reached out to the children during deployment. That could have helped me more during the time.

Even my own boys felt like they were overlooked most of the time by the church. Their dad deployed almost constantly on and off, so I guess it could be easy to think that they were *okay* and didn't need the care or concern of others. Most children (and adults for that matter) are not going to tell people that they want or need attention.

Jacob's Story

I found that many (if not most) of the children of deployed fathers really have had to take on much more responsibility than the average child would have had to encounter. For many, including Jacob, not only did he have to deal with his father being deployed and in harm's way, but he also had to endure many moves during this season in his life. I am including much of his story, as I feel it will really help individuals grasp what it is like to live this life as viewed through his eyes.

Jacob was born in Germany and moved to North Carolina when he was two years old. He is 23 years old, and his father was in the Army for 22 years. Many military brats (children raised in military families) have the privilege of being born out of the country.:

I loved NC and had many dear friends I grew up with. We lived in Fayetteville for 11 years. I never thought my family would move away. Yet, we did. We had to move and I was a very upset brand-new teenager. It was confusing and hard on me as a kid. It was an extreme move. From NC and its 32 degree winters as the low, to NY (Ft. Drum) and its mind numbing -32 degrees with snow falling even in the month of April! North Carolina enjoyed 60's and 70's in April!

I became very depressed. I had lost everything that I had ever known. I was a very serious kid. Things affected me deeply. There were definitely moments of joy that went along with the pain. The snow was pretty freaking awesome since I was just a kid. And I swear where we were in upstate NY that there were more deer than people. I had never seen a deer just walking through my neighborhood and across my driveway before. It was bittersweet. One of the things I began to learn about change was that you have to accept it, because if you do not, then you will be miserable in life.

I was mostly miserable in NY. My family (minus my dad, due to a deployment) then moved to Salem, Oregon when I was 16 years old. Oregon is where my dad is from and he wanted us to be close to his family while he was away. It was upsetting at first because we were led to believe that we would be moving back to NC after our time in NY. Plans changed. Tempers flared, at first. Once in Oregon, and having visited before, it was awesome. Oregon is a beautiful state. The beauty combined with our wonderful relatives was awesome.

I was a difficult teenager, as were four of my seven siblings at the time... and we were all home-schooled! So there was definitely some strife. You can imagine my mom's position. I honestly don't know how she did it alone. The thing is, she wasn't alone. She relied on God's strength and her close friend (my aunt Betsy) to make it through that year without my dad. My dad retired; the decision was to move back to Fayetteville.

My dad deployed to Afghanistan for 6 months after 9/11. I was 13. He then deployed to Seoul, Korea for a year when I was 16. During both of my dad's deployments I was pretty upset. I struggled with much loneliness. I felt like my dad wasn't there for me when I needed him most because of his deployments. I was (and am) always so proud of my dad for his service to our great country, but in my 13 and 16 year-old mind, that just didn't matter so much. He was my dad and should've been at home when I needed him. I always felt like I had to step in and help my mom emotionally, and I always took it upon myself very harshly whenever she was upset or when I'd hear her crying. I didn't know how to deal with it, so it just turned to anger and I either avoided her or argued with her. Things never seemed to make sense back then.

We were part of a somewhat large church in NY when my dad was in Afghanistan. Things seemed normal for a couple of months. The church reminded me of our home church (Manna) back in Fayetteville that we all loved. 'And then' on the local news was our pastor's name and face. The man who led our church in upstate NY was caught stealing money from the church and having an affair with a church member. I became so angry. I was shocked. It hurt me. I learned to never place my trust in man because he will fail you time and time again. I began to learn that the only One who would never fail me was and is Jesus. The church hurt my family. We ended up finding a medium sized non-denominational church in NY that fed us spiritually. It was short lived, as we would soon move to Oregon, but it did help re-establish my love for people and for God's church. While in Oregon, we attended a small 100-person church. My favorite part was when my Dr. Uncle Brian Ray would preach. He helped a lot. He was definitely my dad for that year while my dad was in Korea.

The journey is always most important. Because of our moves I feel like we bonded more as a family. Family is something that cannot be replaced and I have learned to not take the ones I love most for granted. Also, because of the moves, I got to meet and understand many different types of people from different cultures and different coasts. I feel as though I have been able to relate to so many different people from having lived amongst different types. I had to deal with a lot of pain as a kid, things that many people don't have to deal with till later on in life. It definitely helped to prepare me for different trials that I've faced as a young adult. I'm so grateful for my freedom, which comes by the sweat and blood of the men and women who serve in our armed forces. They are the backbone of our great country. And my dad shares in that rich tradition. He will ways be a part of that beautiful group of people who set aside their own interest for the greater interest of others. I have a sincere respect and admiration for such men and women, one that I don't believe would be so strong in me had I not been a part of a military family.

As an end-note, I would encourage all military brats (I say that proudly) to never go it alone. Do not feel like you are alone, because you're not. If you look hard enough, you will find people who genuinely care for you and your spiritual, mental, and physical well-being. We are called to unity and we should join with others arm-in-arm and in love to encourage one another towards a purpose driven life. There is always someone who loves you, as there is also someone who always needs your love.

I have seen such a wisdom and candor in those who have

filled out these surveys, and nothing can relay what they are saying better than their own words. Just reading Jacob's words made me really come to grips with all that my own sons had gone through. Sometimes it takes stepping back and seeing things through the eyes of another person to actually make things a reality for your life and family and bring those times and emotions directly to your heart.

Having raised my own sons in a military lifestyle, I can see many areas that were lacking in their lives, but also many ways that they benefited from their experiences. One thing that is difficult was the lack of roots. Moving frequently can make friendships difficult to maintain. I think this can be the same in children as it is with adults. My sons have very strong relationships that are not just built on convenience. It is more difficult and expensive to maintain these friendships, but the benefits definitely outweigh the cost.

I have also seen an independent spirit in all four of my sons that was spurred on by the necessity to jump-to-the-plate in the areas of responsibility, because their dad was so frequently not at home. I view this aspect as a benefit to their maturity in so many ways. All four of my sons have traveled all around the world on mission trips from a very young age, and I believe that living in a military family and moving so much really gives the children a hunger for other cultures and an ability to see other people as not being different, but special.

My son, Dane, moved away from home the week he turned 18. He didn't depart out of rebellion, but because his entire life had prepared him to be an adult. He is now married with baby number two on the way in a month. He is only 22, but he has accomplished much in his years. He himself has seen the benefits of military living, and has chosen the military path, but with the Coast Guards:

I did it for maritime law enforcement, specialized rates, job opportunities after retirement, family care from the Guard, and locations of units.

The main thing is that it is a life-saving organization. His wife, Kelly, was also raised in a military home. She, too, had to move so frequently and had to be away from her dad often due to deployments and training. This military way of life, although definitely not easy, is not new to her. She has been able to adapt to any location. In the short amount of time Dane and Kelly have been together, they have lived in four different states. Kelly sees it as an adventure, and they are truly making the most of all of the opportunities they encounter.   I see this new generation as strengthened by the trials they have been through. So many that I have spoken to have really seen their experiences while being in a military family as something that has caused them to a maturity beyond their years.

Moving is something that is most often not easy for most adults. For many military children, moving is just a way of life. Megan, 22, says:

Moving around was never too difficult for me as I was home schooled, so I was never the new kid in school or anything like that. I also made friends very easily; and usually we lived around other families that moved a lot too, so all of my friends and I sort of knew that sooner or later one of us would be moving. It was still usually sad saying goodbye to those friends, but I suppose knowing it would happen eventually made it less of a big deal. All around, it never had a negative effect on me. I enjoyed going somewhere new after a while. My mother tells me that I used to translate basic German sentences for her when we went shopping. I don't remember any of that at all.

That was an EXTREMELY exciting part of my life and I still think about it pretty often actually. My sister, Becca, was really blonde back then, and in Korea it's good luck to rub a blonde person's head, so she was always getting pat on the head by Koreans everywhere we went. When we first got there it scared her, but by the time we left she didn't notice at all when it happened. Basically I really enjoyed living overseas, and am now extremely grateful for all of the countries I have either lived in or visited. I consider it a privilege to have been so many places that some people only ever dream of seeing, and to have learned at an early age how diverse and amazing the wide world can actually be.

Megan has also been on several missions trips overseas, and I have observed many military children really have that urge to go to other countries and help those that are less fortunate than they are. I believe that they are able to acclimate to the change of culture and climate much more easily than someone who has lived the same place his or her entire life. I also think it's not just the desire to visit other places. Because they have lived in a military family and have not always had a *normal* life, many military children are able to recognize when someone else is hurting and have the desire to help those less fortunate than they are.

Megan has lived in Germany, Korea, and several states. Her father deployed for a short duration to Desert Storm in the 1990's when she was much younger. Megan feels that being raised in a military family has truly benefited her as a person:

There is so much I am grateful about having been raised in the military. I have never felt scared of people who are not like me, I have never taken for granted all the blessings that I have in my life and in America as a nation, I have never disrespected a man or woman who is willing to die for my freedom, and I have never worried that I am missing out on the world. I have learned that absence does not mean forgetting and that distance does not entail a lack of love or commitment. I have learned how much I value time with the people I love, and I have learned the importance of refusing to let pettiness or anger or drama or anything like that steal more time with the people I love away from me. I have had adventures and experiences that will be with me always, and I have met people and seen places that still grip my heart. I have grown to respect my father and be thankful for my mother, to always be for my sister and on her side and to trust that my parents and my God will always be for me and on my side. Any ill experience I had growing up as an army brat is severely shadowed by everything I gained from all of i

The only advice I feel sure enough to share with anyone trying to raise a military family is that, as cliché and overstated it may sound, trusting in God is the single greatest decision you can make. ALWAYS trust that God will carry you. ALWAYS trust that God will provide and care for you. ALWAYS trust that God is madly in love with you and completely understands you. ALWAYS put your faith in Him and He will not fail you.

Military moves affected Alice in a different way than they did Megan. Alice is also 22 and her dad was in the military 21 years:

I think that between our moves and the moving-away that many of my early friends did, it kind of skewed how I viewed friendships. It made it hard to make friends with anyone nearby. I simply kept pen-pals for years instead.

Jihan was very much affected by the moves that her family made all throughout her life. Even still, this has caused her to be able to acclimate to moving much easier than if she had lived in one location her whole life:

I feel like I moved often. I was born in Oregon and lived there until I was seven; moved to Ft. Hood, Texas when my Dad went active duty; moved to Schofield Barracks, HI; Ft. Campbell, KY; and Fort Hood, TX (yet again!). That was the last duty station that I was at with my parents. I then went on to move on my own several times and become a nomad myself. Not only did we move to several duty stations, we also moved several times while at the duty station. I did not enjoy moving around. When I was younger I used to wish that I lived in one place my whole life and grew up with the same friends. It was very hard to move every few years and have to make new friends (knowing I most likely would never see my old friends again) and finding a routine again. It seemed like right when things started to feel 'normal' we would up and move.

Jihan is 25 years old now, and her dad deployed three times within a four year span, starting when she was 14 years old. Both she and Alice have this in common regarding the times that their dad deployed: They enjoyed that time with their moms.

I did not want my dad to be in harm's way, but honestly I liked it when he deployed. That might sound horrendous but at that time, both of my sisters had gotten married and it was just my parents and myself. When my dad would deploy I felt like my mom and I had more fun. It was just the two of us and we could do whatever we wanted, whenever we wanted and not have to run anything past my dad. Sometimes after my mom would pick me up from school, we would go to Sonic and get a fun drink and split onion rings. We wouldn't have done that with my dad. Even when it came to buying groceries we would buy fun 'girl' food and have special treats. I liked spending the extra time with my mom, admits Jihan.

Alice would agree with Jihan's comments: *I actually was more comfortable with how things were when my dad was gone, for the most part. He intimidates me and I never really knew how to respond to him or open up to him. My mom and brother would fight when he's gone, but all three seem to have disagreements now.*

Deployments are definitely difficult, and each individual, adult or child, will cope in whatever way they can to make life more bearable. It's not an easy thing to have a member of your family gone for extended periods of time, and I know that for myself as an adult I would rationalize things in my head to sort of fool myself into looking forward to that time my husband would be gone. I would plan projects around the house, plan trips to go on for which I had no time were my husband not there as well as other things. Looking back, I can see that this behavior was definitely a coping mechanism. Although I don't think it was a bad thing, I think that if I would continue on in that mindset, I could have caused a wedge in our family. Thankfully I do realize these things and switch back to being thankful that my husband is home when he *is* home!

One thing that I recognize within my own sons was how close they became to each other due to all that they went through. After reading through what so many of the other military brats wrote, I see that it was a common factor. It is definitely a benefit to the military life. Says Rebecca, 18, who is Megan's younger sister:

At one point my neighbor, Blane, moved the toy car while

I was still in the tree. I sat there yelling at him telling him to put it back until I saw my older sister get up, walk over, punch him, and put the car back so I could get down. That was the first time I truly admired my sister. She has such a bold personality and a powerful attitude. I couldn't help but love someone as strong as she was protective over me. I know now the attitude siblings take on when they see one another in distress, but at the time she had saved me and put my car back in it's place. It was amazing! Of course, I've noticed over time that military families see the importance in what family really is, and they look after one another. It's just a talent that is acquired through the years.

Megan would agree with what her sister said regarding family and being there for one another:

Whenever my dad would go out to the field I remember getting a bit more protective of my sister. It wasn't that Dad being gone worried me, or that my mom acted scared and caused me to panic. I just knew in my kid mind that if Dad wasn't home to take care of my sister, then it was double time my job to take care of her.

I have seen with my own eyes the close connection of so many siblings who are part of a military family. I also believe it is often due to the fact that often they are so far from the rest of the extended family that the bond of the immediate family because very tight-knit.

Her sister, Rebecca, has this to add:

One of the biggest things I've noticed with my family specifically is how tightly woven the four of us have become in my lifetime.

Something about knowing the dynamics of what it's like to be a part of a family that is a part of something so important for our country brings us all together. The patriotism in these kids and the fact that they know what their fathers are fighting for, makes me realize that the understanding of what a hero is will not die out in this generation.

I also asked these kids how they felt churches helped their families or what could have been done differently to meet their needs. There was a wide range of answers both negative and positive. Many felt that the church really helped their families get through the tough times. Dylan's dad was in the Army for 20 years and was either deployed or in training most of his growing up years. He is 15 years old now caused both him and his brothers to a work at a higher standard around the house to help their mom during the frequent times their dad was gone. Dylan had great things to say about how his church was there for them while their dad was not there:

Yes, my family was in a church during the time that our father was deployed. We kept the same church during the time that he was being deployed, and I feel as if it helped by giving me an amazing amount of friends to be with, and a fantastic feeling of confidence that my dad was going to be alright.

Dylan has much good to say about being raised in a military family:

Positive outcomes that came from being a military family include being open-minded to new experiences, whether far from home or not, and most importantly, to stay strong during hard times, because everything will turn out just fine. Most importantly, I have learned to stay strong and move on at all times from this experience and many others. I would say that this has had a good impact on my life and perspective of living, and nothing can bring me down.

Some of the Challenges of Being a Military Brat

Not everyone has had a positive experience in the church, whether adult or child. Alice, who was raised in the church and whose dad was frequently either deployed overseas or in training, had this to say about her church experience:

I was part of the church during those times. Whether or not it helped is hard to say. I'm honestly at a point of disassociating myself with the church. I never really felt at home there. I felt like there was an expectation of who I was supposed to be that never lined up with who I was and who I could ever honestly be.

This is unfortunately a common occurrence in many young adults: not just those growing up in military families. I believe that the church must be not only meeting the needs of the people, but it must be relevant to the people to whom they are reaching. Alice really felt like the church was often just trying to appeal to people's emotions, and it was not balanced in the area of teaching her about the Bible and showing her the relevance of how that would apply to her life. Everyone is really searching for significance. If churches don't show people how relevant and real Jesus is, it's almost a guarantee that their search will continue elsewhere. We, as the church, really need to be aware of the needs of the people around us, because we are supposed to be a shining light of how to love people as God loves. Rebecca has this to say about her church experience,:

When I was younger, the church helped develop a deep understanding of God's love and goodness to me. It showed me that our God is a loving one rather than a ruthless one. The church showed me that what I had was a gift. From having such a loving father, I quickly saw and understood the love I was receiving from God. I wish every young girl could say that about their dads. I guess that's why I truly know what I have is a gift. But when I started to get older, I also started to develop my own relationship and opinion about God and religion. Every now and then, I would disagree with someone on something they were telling me and instead of respecting the differences in our relationships with God, they made me feel condemned. A few times I got remarks on how my family specifically liked to just disagree with people. Don't get me wrong, I love that church and the pastor that leads it, but I could see I had outgrown some of the people. I hope not to bash this wonderful growing place.

Because Joanna's father was a chaplain, her church experience when she was living at home was often limited to the Chapel:

Since my dad is a Chaplain, we were generally a part of whatever service he was assigned to. Occasionally, we would attend a church outside of the Chapel. It was hard for me to connect to anyone my age as the services seemed to have more young families or single soldiers, so I tended to keep to myself. I wish I could have met (at the time) more kids my age or have been involved in some kind of youth group. When we moved to Hawaii, we still attended the Chapel services but also started going to another church that we were affiliated with. It was a small church, but loving, and we all became very close (like family) In fact, I still go to it today!

Joanna not only grew up in a military home, but she wound up marrying a man in the military. They met in Hawaii, had to move to Maryland for a few years, and now they are back in Hawaii.

Many of the military brats really felt that the churches they were part of really met their needs as a military family. It wasn't the fact that these churches had a specific program for the military. They simply had things set up that really benefited the military in their congregation. Says Keith, 20, who was born in Italy, and whose dad was frequently gone:

We were really active in being part of the church body. Both of my brothers and I went to the youth group while my mother attended a small-group Bible study that was hosted by another church family in their home. Whenever a military member was deployed, we would tie a yellow ribbon around an American flag and display it in the front of the church. We prayed over them when they left, while they were gone, and whenever we felt led to do so individually. The church leadership always made sure they had help of all kinds available to the families of those deployed. It definitely made a difference; we had at least three or four families with husbands gone at a time. Aside from constantly providing fellowship and showing the love of Christ, the church did everything in they could to care for us.

Jihan said:

I think the church was helpful. There was one church member who ran a lawn care business and would mow our lawn in the summertime while my dad was deployed. It was a big yard and he had a riding lawn mower, which was definitely preferable to our push mower with those muggy Kentucky summers. There was also a Bible study that the church had called W.O.W., which stood for Wives of Warriors, for women who had husbands in the military. I babysat their children while they went to Bible study. I can't say that I babysat for altruistic purposes (I was a teenager after all and I needed some sweet moolah), but I think that was probably helpful for the women to feel supported and understood by other women in similar circumstances and to be able to have an hour or two where they could interact with other adults and have their children looked after.

Even though they would all admit that it was difficult for them growing up with their father's frequently gone, most can really see the benefits of growing up in a military family. Keith says:

Being in a military family has definitely been a positive experience. Having moved to a few different places, I've made friends all over Tennessee and the East Coast. I have since then decided to join the Air Force, and I feel part of that has to do with having grown up around the military; everywhere you go, you're part of a community that understands you, for the most part, and will go out of their way to help you.

Joshua is 17 years old, and his father has been in the military over 22 years. Although he has never had to move, he does realize that living in a military family is different than living in a civilian family:

When you are a child in an army home one positive is that you learn structure and how to work hard. Having a dad who can be sometimes strict because of the training can be annoying when you are younger, but when you get older and look back you are glad for all he made you do. It made me more responsible and gave me a lot of life skills many people whose parents are not in the military don't have.

I have also found that for military children moving is something to which they are able to adapt in their adult life. It's not such a huge ordeal to them, as they have grown up doing this often, and know what to expect.

Of my two sons who have already moved out, one is living in California, and the other is living in Virginia. Although I would consider them very connected to one another, they are still able to follow after their dreams and move wherever they feel led to move. Jihan would agree:

I was able to live, and visit, places I would never have been able to if my dad had a regular civilian job. Hawaii will always have a special place in my heart and I feel very fortunate to have spent several formative years of my childhood there.

She has lived and traveled all over the world both while in the military and doing missions work after she moved out of the house:

Growing up in the military also made me able to embrace change. The thought of moving doesn't freak me out, since I don't have any real roots anywhere. I am not scared to try new things or to go to different places. I was also able to meet many people, while many were only in my life briefly, a few have remained dear friends that I know I will keep for the rest of my life.

She has now recently transplanted herself, her husband and their new baby from Pennsylvania to Oregon.

The song *That's What Soldiers Do* by Monk and Neagle really expresses what the heart of a Christian soldier should be in his relationship with the Lord and with his family. The lyrics depict a soldier getting ready to be sent out to war, and he is singing to his oldest son. Monk and Neagle have always been one of my favorite bands, but this song is just something that tugs at my heart and makes me cry almost every time I hear it (You can easily find it on Youtube).

The soldier in these lyrics realizes that his battle is not just for the military but that he is also a warrior for Christ. He really exhorts his son in this and encourages him to be all that God has called him to be. One of the most important things that this song shows is that everything we do, whether we are a soldier or not, is for love. This is so true in parenting. Everything we do for our children should be because we love them. And we should teach our children to love the way that Christ loves us, which is unconditionally.

Tips from Chapter 13

• If you know a child of a deployed father, be extra sensitive to his or her needs, spoken and unspoken. Most often they don't even know what they need. Ask them how they are doing, and take the time to really stop and listen. Children know when you are asking out of genuine concern as opposed to asking because you just think it's what you should be doing. Be genuinely concerned and attentive to their answers.

• If you have children of your own of similar age and same gender, get with your children and see what you can do to include the kids in what you do as a family. If your husband is not deployed and they have a teen son or pre-teen, see if you can include them in a guy activity so they are not only having to do what their mom and siblings are doing. Boys need their guy time and guy input.

• Ask the military spouse if there is anything that she would like you to do to help her with her children. If she has teens, maybe she needs help with homework that she may struggle with. Perhaps she needs help if they are learning how to drive. Ask the mom, and as always, wait for a reply!

Questions from Chapter 13

• Are you a mom whose husband is deployed or gone to a school or training? Are you making sure you are spending the extra time that your children need with you? Do you realize that they cannot process their needs as maturely as you can. And because you are the only one at home, it is up to you to make sure they feel secure and safe?

• If you belong to a church, how are they keeping track of the needs of the military families that have a deployed parent? Is there anything that you can do to possibly create a list and find out what the needs of the families back home are?

• If your husband is deployed, are you making sure that

your oldest is not taking on too much responsibility? Responsibility is a good thing. But when there is pressure and and too much responsibility placed on the child, the child could become resentful or possibly not have enough time for homework or extracurricular activities that could also help him or her to mature.

POINTS YOU WANT TO REMEMBER

feel free to jot down notes below...

- C H A P T E R 1 4 -

How Churches Can Help

Bear one another's burdens, and so fulfill the law of Christ.

Galatians 6:2

Based off of personal experience and the experience of others, I've compiled a list of things that most military women with deployed husbands would enjoy *not* hearing from others:

• *Don't* tell me that you know how I feel, if you don't.

• *Don't* say that you'll be praying for me and my family unless you really are planning to pray.

• *Don't* tell me that you'll be there for me and help me when I need it unless this is really your intent. It would be better if you didn't say anything than to get my hopes up.

• If I ask for prayer, *don't* tell me not to worry and that my husband will be okay. First of all, I asked for prayer, not a lecture. Second of all, who is anyone to say that someone will be okay unless God told him directly? Deployed husbands are at war, and their lives are at stake.

• *Don't* assume that I don't need help, because my husband deploys frequently and I can handle it. The more frequent the deployments, the more needs I have.

• *Don't* assume that I have more free time because my husband is not home. Quite the opposite is true, because I am now acting as a single parent.

- If you know my birthday, please, *don't* forget it. You may be the only family that I have nearby.

- *Don't* assume that I have a place to go for the holidays. Many military families, ours included, have always lived very far from family. Unless someone invited us over or we invited others over, our holidays were spent alone without my husband or my kids' dad.

- *Don't* ask me to do childcare at church. I just might go whacko on you!

That is just a short list of things that have bugged me during my husband's deployments. Of course, every wife is different, and the need of every family is different. I know many women who have family nearby and get plenty of help. It still doesn't mean that it's easy with a spouse being gone, and the uncertainty of their return. But for those who have no family nearby (raises hand up high!), those needs are amplified.

Sherry's Prayer

These are heartfelt writings of a lifelong friend of mine. Sherry's family and ours met almost 20 years ago when our husbands were stationed at Ft. Lewis, Washington. We have both traveled a similar circle around the United States and for this season are living in the same city in Texas. Her husband has deployed countless times, and she was asked several years ago to write about her thoughts regarding prayer for deployed soldiers. She writes from a place deep within her heart that many of us who have gone through the affects of a deployment can comprehend. The words Sherry uses really put into perspective some of the unique situations that both the soldier and his family left behind face.

Basically without prayer and my dependence on God to get me through every long day (especially knowing they were on a mission and couldn't' hear from them for days on end) I would have lost my mind. When we knew someone was killed and they would shut down all communications on purpose so nothing would leak back before families were notified... prayer on what the hell I could possibly say to my friend and lieutenant's wife when we went to tell her that her husband had been shot and killed by a sniper. Oddly enough prayer at that time, especially for her, was the only safety net of escape from a pain that is so surreal and seemingly unbearable. The fear and looming thoughts of the possibility that your loved one may not come home doesn't creep into the night once again and rob you of sleep for the umpteenth time in months requires deep prayer. Praying to God as you turn the corner and see the familiar tan government van with a chaplain driving and another uniformed officer that's driving down the street as you hold your breath that it doesn't stop in front of your best friend's house or worse... yours.

I pray to God that he would take care of my husband, knowing that he is going on a seven- day mission in 140 temp with only enough water for 3 days. Prayers are needed for the soldiers that were coming home to surprise their spouses that they are not going to get their own surprise when they walk into their house to find their wife sleeping with some schmuck and praying that he was smart enough to not let her have access to ALL his hard earned work and money.

Prayers are needed for the children of the hundreds of divorced couples after such a horrendous sacrifice for our country. Prayers are needed for myself because every time I see a middle eastern man that I don't carry hatred and bitterness in my heart. Prayers are needed for my strong and loving husband that he comes home and then when he does he can still function like a normal person and not have depression or PTSD so badly that he shuts down completely and it ends up destroying our marriage anyhow.

I need prayers for my very own children that the absence of their father will not scar them for life and that I can be a strong and loving enough mother that can sustain them through such a time so they can still live life with fond and happy memories of their childhood. Last but not least I need to be thankful in my prayers for his safety, his return, for the millions of prayers from others, for my friends and family that supported me and were by my side, grateful for my best friend that understood why I couldn't leave the

*house for a day because all I could do was cry; trying to
pull myself together before my children came home.
Graciously she would make us dinner and bring it to the
house. I guess you can safely say that 'prayer' is all we had,
all of us, something seemingly so simple, a few words
uttered, moaned, cried out, whispered... the glue. The words
we lifted to God, Jesus, and the Holy Spirit were the glue
that held me, my family, my friends, co spouses, together in
broken, shattered moments of the worst news one could
possibly bare: when a friend found out her husband was
killed by a sniper. Prayer was the only thing that comes to
mind, even for the unbeliever. Thank God for our
communication pathway to god and thanks be to Him for
listening.*

I have noticed vast changes in the last 10 years in how
people respond to wives and families with spouses deployed.
Soon after September 11, 2001 when my husband first
deployed to the Middle East, many friends and family would
call me to see how Mike was doing, how I was doing, and
how the boys were doing. It was a national tragedy, and the
images of the planes crashing into the buildings were fresh
on everyone's minds. I belonged to a church where my
husband was the only one in the unit he was serving, so for
awhile he was the only one deployed. It was a very difficult
time for me, as I felt alone in what I was going through, and I
felt that no one could really relate. Nothing like this had ever
happened before, so no one knew to ask if I needed help. To
me it seemed obvious, with four young sons and living
thousands of miles from our closest relatives, I definitely
needed help. After several months we became friends with an
older retired Navy couple that formed a care group to help
out the families. This was such a helpful operation, which I
took advantage of immensely. This sweet couple are now
like adopted parents to us, and I'm sure they fulfill that role
to several other couples.

There are many needs for families of deployed soldiers as
well as families where the soldier is not away. There are
always more needs when the spouse is deployed, because
there is only one parent on hand for the children. I would say

that women whose husbands are deployed geographically would be considered single parents. The women have the burdens on their shoulders of being the heads of their households and taking care of the needs that both the wife and husband would do together.

How Individuals Can Help Military Families

When you see a wife whose husband is gone, see how she is doing and just ask how things are. Because my husband is deployed so often (8 times in under 11 years), most people assumed it's easy for me and that I didn't need any help because I go through this all the time. During the last deployment, very few people in leadership at our church even asked me how Mike was doing. Sadly, I had come to expect this based upon previous deployments, and I find that the more often he is gone the less people will ask about him and the less help they assume I will need. *Do not make this assumption* if you want to minister to the needs of military families. Make sure you are reaching their children, too. It seems that all of my sons have had a few special men in their lives who have really reached out to them during deployments. This has been a Godsend to my family and much appreciated. Being a father to the fatherless is something that is lacking in Western society as a whole, and we the church need to fulfill that role. Being present for these kids (especially boys) who need other males to be a an example to them that they can see regularly (and who they can talk when needed) is so much more important than people realize.

One of the greatest needs we have when our husbands are deployed is help around the home with basic fixing of things like the car, yard, and appliances. It's not necessary that the church provided the church or individuals free of charge, but most military families are not living in their hometown. So a list of who is trustworthy, whose prices are fair, who would offer military discounts, and who would be available during non-business hours would be extremely helpful. Such a list provided by churches when new members attend would be beneficial. Often, there are individuals in the church who would be willing to help with some of the easier tasks which would putt less of a financial burden on military families for something that may be simple for some but not so much for others.

Let me interject here with a very important fact that many don't seem to understand: *we wives are asking for help, but often merely get someone saying Oh that's too bad. I'll pray for you.* Prayer is fine and wonderful, *but Jesus was moved by compassion, and that compassion caused Him to take action like the church should take action.* When He saw the hungry, He fed them. When He saw the sick, He healed them. When He saw those in distress, He comforted them. We need to be doing the same for the military families, not just saying a quick prayer and then sending them on their way.

Ideas for Churches to Help Military Families

There are so many needs that military families have. Have *grandparents* for the families. Pair up the military families with an older couple that can function as adopted parents and grandparents. If the church you attend is mainly made up of military families (I believe ours was about 80% or more military), that may not be an option. If your church is a part of a larger congregation due to denomination or other, see if one of the other churches can be of help to your church in any of the ways mentioned.

Once a month having a Mom's-Day-Out is a great opportunity to help mothers with deployed husbands. The youth in the church, young adults etc. could volunteer their time to help in something like this. It should not be an occasion where the moms have to take turns babysitting each other's kids. At the same time if there are teens whose fathers are deployed, make sure these teens are *not* included in the volunteering, unless they absolutely want to volunteer. Deployments are so difficult on the children, and they don't need another burden heaped on them.

My family was a part of two separate church congregations during the ten-year time period that my husband deployed. As much as these organizations seemed to want to help the military families, there was one thing that both churches did: *they expected the military families to help the military families.* While it is true that military families may know what their needs are, that does not mean that they are able to fulfill those needs. This just adds more pressure to the families who already have so much they are juggling. The needs are so great with spouses deployed, that the women don't need to have even more stressful responsibility. If people in the church who are not military families would offer their time to find out what the needs of the military families are and then help them even in the simplest of ways, then the military families will be much less burdened.

Often when someone in a church presents a need to those in leadership, they tell the person that it is now their ministry because they brought up. *This should never be the case.* If one were to have a need in a particular area, it does not qualify that person to start a ministry to meet that need in other people. That seems too often to be the case in churches, causing the women of deployed husbands to lead ministries that reach out to other women in similar circumstances, whether or not they are qualified.

Holidays are especially difficult with a spouse gone. Many wives have family nearby and can visit them during holidays, but there are also very many who are left behind. It is a lonely time for the women and children without the husband and fathers around, so try to put yourself and your family in their shoes and treat them like you'd want to be treated: invite them over for the holidays, not assuming that others already have included them. For our family holidays were often very sad and lonely times. Our closest family was thousands of miles away, and we were almost never invited to anyone's house. I would hear from the church pulpit how church was family, but in reality I was never invited to anyone's house for the holiday or most often not even for meals, unless I was the one doing the inviting. This was very hurtful and disappointing for our family. Sometimes people would even say they would have the family over once my husband comes home. I guess they figured that my boys and I only needed to eat when my husband was home!

Input from Other Military Wives

After writing about what I personally think churches and

individuals can do to help the families, I realized that it would be good to get input from other military wives: many of them. So I sent out a survey to almost 100 military wives or ex-military wives. These women live and have lived all over the world, and I wanted to have more information than just my own personal experiences in order to share them with everyone. It was eye-opening to read all of the surveys and the heartache that many have gone through. So many solutions seem quite simple, and I really believe a change can and must be made so that military families will get the help and support that they need.

FRG's

When asking the wives whether or not they utilize the FRG (Family Readiness Group) that is available to them through their husband's individual units, the answers varied. Some of the women were very active in their FRG's, even helping to lead in some fashion. Most, however, did not have time nor did they feel comfortable sharing with this support system. Many found that these meetings were quite cliquey and there was more gossip than help going on. Having lived in many places and having dealt with many support groups, I think that all of the above is true. As with any situation, one has to be wise with what she shares and to who she shares it.

For many, it wasn't a matter of not wanting nor agreeing with their FRG leaders or information given at meetings, it was more a matter of not having the time. Most of these women find their greatest support in their Christian friends. Vanessa, whose husband was active military for 10 years said:

While in the military, support was hard to come by. I really felt the support come from my church more than anything else.

I have found this to be the case with many of the women with whom I have spoken. They are more likely to go to their church, which they can trust and count on as family for their support, rather than their Family Readiness Group.

Ellen has almost the exact same thing to say about where her support comes from:

My support has always come from my church/friends.

Ellen remembers a time when many husbands deployed and one of the women started a quilting group to help support the younger women whose husbands were gone. This wonderful woman was none other than the wonderful Wendie who I spoke of earlier as being a *Mom* to me. She has impacted many women with her loving and reaching life.

Christine, whose husband had been in the military for over 21 years and has recently retired had this to say (and I believe this may have been the most common response to this question that I encountered):

My involvement with family support groups through the years was minimal. They were helpful during times of deployment, as a point of contact when I was unable to contact my husband as to his whereabouts and times of departures and arrivals. I did not have any negative experiences with family support groups, I just found more support from my church family.

I find that my involvement FRG's was similar to Christine's. There was one group of women that were part of my husband's team during two of his deployments to Iraq. I guess they would be referred to as Team Wives,and not so much Family Readiness Groups. I still remain in contact with these women. Because our husbands were often in harm's way and were like brothers to each other with all that they were going through, it formed a bond between us that may not have been there had we just met without these circumstances. We would often get together, play games, eat, and just enjoy each other's company. Knowing that we were all in the same boat gave us a common group that wouldn't have necessarily been there otherwise. I am thankful that I have formulated these friendships, because based on our separate lifestyles (some without kids, differing ages…) we may have not have met one another.

There are also several women who have been very involved in their FRG's and have found them extremely supportive. I believe that this is truly how the FRG's are supposed to be working. I was more involved in our military support groups before we moved to Tennessee, and my husband deployed so frequently. I was busy raising my four sons as a *single* mom and didn't have time to be very involved when Mike was away so often. When we lived in other locations, my time was not as limited so that I was able to help out more in this area. I have found that the support groups in any location we have lived have been extremely helpful. When my son's appendix ruptured, I had a leader come in with gifts for Rainier and even a toy for our new baby pug! The rear detachment (the person who is in charge of handling everything when the soldiers are deployed) even called and visited us in the hospital to make sure all of our needs were met.

Keri has also had great experience with her FRG in the past,:

We moved to Clarksville, TN in 2000. When we first arrived to TN I was involved with the FRG that his unit provided. It was very new for me being a military wife and I did not know anyone. I had never left my hometown so when we got married and moved away it was very difficult for me. The company my husband was in was very close. The wives on the team were very helpful and friendly. We did a lot of outings together with and without our husbands. I believe at that time I really needed that support from them, since I was not involved in a church. We would go to each other when we needed something or talk about our problems.

Once Keri started going to church and became more involved in her church, her need for the FRG was not as significant. But, as I have also found, it's not necessary for the church to have something specifically for military families as long as the needs are met by the people:

I think it is important that the church is aware of the military families in their church. The church I attended for five years did not have a special program for military, but I was fine without it because I had close relationships and didn't feel I needed it. We did change the last year to a different church where there were a couple of programs for the military. It didn't matter either way for me because I had friends in and out of the military. I think that it would help other families connect better and feel more comfortable talking about issues because they have gone through same issues.

This is saying much, because Keri's needs at the time were great:

Previously I was married for six years and he passed away from a brain tumor in 2006 while actively serving in the Army. I was 27 years old when we got married and he was in the military for 14 years. He served in the United States Army and in Special Forces. He was in the SIF Company in 5th Group.

Her husband had to come home from deployments due to his health issues, and they had many family needs. Her church had really pulled through to help take care of their situation in his life and in his passing. Keri is now remarried to a wonderful man, who is also in the military, and they have one daughter and another daughter on the way. She has been an example to many military wives of one who has become even stronger through the calamity she has endured.

One of the greatest issues that came to the surface upon reading the surveys that all of the women shared with me was the need for help with the children when the husbands were deployed. The mom is acting as the mother *and* the father and is most often completely overwhelmed when it comes not only to dealing with being a dual parent but also to handling the fears and abandonment issues that their children may face when their dads are at war. This is something that I really believe should be a major priority of churches, as the church is supposed to be filling the roll of the family. Unfortunately, I have not found this to be the case in most instances. I do believe that many churches say and believe that they are acting as family, but too often they don't realize the incredible need that the military family has, especially when the spouse is deployed. I don't know if this is a greater need where boys are concerned, but there really seems to be a huge lack in the churches of men who will stand by and reach out to the boys who are left behind. I know this personally as I have 4 sons who have witnessed this.

Jessica from Tennessee who has two young boys says:

Mostly the church has provided care so I could come to church. I have those crazy kids that quiet moms look at with fear. They run, scream, punch, fall down, hurt themselves and jump up and do it again! They scare people. But that is how God made them. They are growing and learning and it's my job to shape them into little humans that can survive in this world... but in the mean time it isn't pretty.

Being able to go to church and feel comfortable that my kids are safe is the biggest help. I know that they will be clean and alive when church is over. That is the goal at least. The church had to step back from providing childcare for most of our growth groups. That was hard. Especially when my husband was deployed. I had to line up childcare so that i could go to a group and that stopped me from leading a group as well. Without anyone to fall back on while raising children makes it hard to commit to anything...who knows who will get sick or throw a fit and make you late. Right now my job is my kids, they are my number one disciples.

Christine from Tennessee has two children who are now in their 20's. She says:

When my husband was away, I desired a man from the church to spend time with my son. I asked about 3 different men about being this kind of mentor and nothing really became of it. I do recall feeling let down in this.

Having someone step in as a big brother or big sister for the children when one of the parents is deployed is one of the greatest needs to which I found the wives replying in the survey. They are so often overlooked, and their need for someone to step in and fill that roll is not very common. I do have a friend, Bill, who would take his friend's daughters to the father/daughter ball that we had in our city. This was very touching to all who witnessed, but more importantly, it meant the world to the girls. Vanessa from Alabama who has 5 children had a lot of input regarding the children issue. Vanessa had been part of several different churches due to military moves. Here are a few of the informative statements she made:

One huge thing I see lacking for the kids is big brothers and sisters coming in and being a buddy to these kids who need extra men or women in their lives.

And Vanessa also had a sad but true remark regarding teens. I believe this is not just for teens of military families, but I see this being the case for teens in general:

Sometimes I think the adults don't think that these teens want to communicate with them and the sad thing is they need it.

So many times people don't realize what the needs are for the teens, because they most often won't voice them. They are looked upon as rebellious when they are simply just being quiet. Often for those who have a parent who is deployed, it's so important that adults really go out of their way to show their concern and care. This has been something that the parents and teens themselves have voiced is lacking. It has caused a lot of pain, and some teens have even made the decision not to belong to a church at all due to feeling judged and uncared for.

Marie has eight children (four from her previous marriage) to a Special Forces soldier, and four children from her current husband. Her reply was short and to the point:

I don't think our church did much to help the children during the deployment. I received my support from personal friends.

I have found that many women do receive most of their help when their husbands are deployed from friends, and not the church directly.

I believe it is wonderful to have that support of great friends like that, but it's equally important that the church meet the needs of their congregation. This is especially necessary for military families, because when they are moving frequently they don't get to take their friends with them from place to place (or their extended family), so it's very important that the church fill in as that family.

Cheryl from Louisiana has seven children. Although her husband has never deployed in the 20 years, he's been in the military and she still can grasp the needs that would occur:

I think a spouse at home would need help with the kids, maybe a night out to herself, or a day to get her hair or nails done. Offers to help around the house with handyman stuff, or the car. Prayers in person or over the phone for her husband's safety and her peace/children's peace.

Yes, prayer is a huge need for the military families! There is so much unseen turmoil when a spouse is deployed, and prayer is such and important and often overlooked need for these families. The families are in need of prayer before, during, and after the whole deployment cycle. They also need to know that people are praying for them. A mere *We're praying for you* will not work.

Emily, who has three small daughters and whose husband deploys regularly would agree:

Prayer and frequent positive talk about daddy and what he does would most help my daughters. My oldest daughter's children's church teacher taught her class about what her daddy does and encouraged them to pray for her. She also let her know that she is a hero, too.

I don't think that prayer for the military families can be stressed enough. This is true with families where the spouse deploys and where the spouse remains in the country. Almost every single wife whom I questioned said that prayer is one of the number one things that individuals and churches can do to help their families. Vanessa agrees:

I think for me the biggest and most important support was the prayers of those around me.

Sarah from Tennessee has 2 daughters. Her husband began deploying soon after they were married. In between one of the deployments, they had their second daughter:

I honestly didn't feel like the church helped my children through the deployments. I saw people on Sunday and growth group night. Other than that I was on my own. I want to say that I am not at all offended, partly because I feel like it was up to me to ask for help if I needed it. I felt like I was burden if I did ask someone for help with my kids. Especially when someone says hey if you ever need childcare call me. Then when you did make the call they didn't answer nor return the call. I just took care of my girls on my own. I think there should be programs in church like big brother/sister programs. People that have the extra time pick a family or two that they could dedicate a little extra time to. That would help a military mom out so much!

Something that is very common in churches (and even more often seen in military couples) is that one spouse goes to church and the other one prefers not to attend. There are many reasons for this, but a common factor is that often the wives will come to church and deepen their commitment to their faith while their husbands are deployed. Often the women are welcomed into the church with open arms and feel like they have found their new family. This can cause much strife when the husband comes back after being gone for an extended period because it makes him feel like an outsider. It's imperative that the church really makes an effort to reach out to these men and be relevant to them. Men and women have different needs and ways of thinking, and the church often only appeals to women. My husband and I have seen churches filled with women, because the needs of warmth and nurturing are available to them. But many churches really lack in the area of showing the strength, power, and relevance of an authentic Christian life.

Savanna is a young wife whose husband frequently deploys. He goes on shorter deployments (generally one to two months at a time), but several times a year. He is deployed as often as he is home. Savanna grew up in the church and has a strong foundation in her faith:

We used to go to church at the beginning of our marriage until my husband decided he didn't believe in God anymore, and we stopped going. I never established a good enough church home to feel comfortable going on my own so I just pray and cry out to God constantly to have the marriage I've always prayed for that is centered in God. Until then, my church is in my heart where I try to keep hope that my husband will find faith again.

Her husband also grew up in the church, but he now claims that he doesn't believe in God at all. His lack of belief is based on the inconsistencies in the lives of other soldiers who claim to be Christians:

My husband's outlook on the church is that he thinks a lot of the men he works with that are Christians are hypocrites. Actually, he feels most are. But a lot of the men that have tried to reach out to him in the past have sort of burned some bridges with him either from talking about him behind his back, looking at porn, or just having an attitude that you wouldn't expect from these men. He has a hard time accepting that people are the same person in church as they are day-to-day.

Unfortunately, this is the norm in most military men. Many go to church on Sundays, but then when they are with their fellow soldiers they are completely different. If the church can get a grasp of how common this is, then the church would see the need to really train and equip these soldiers in the spiritual battles that they face in the work place.

David is a seasoned Army veteran and has been on many deployments, taking him away from his family for numerous stretches of time. He knows the needs that his family had while he was deployed and has some great tidbits of advice for how churches could help the military families:

Take the time to consider the families Don't get so wrapped up in the ministry of self or church exaltation but serve individuals. Provide personal, marital, and family counseling. Help and personally acknowledge families of deployed soldiers, not just in public. Get to know the families. This is tough in churches in military towns, and it shouldn't be assumed that it is being done. Be a stand-in-father or develop programs for boys and or girls who have fathers and mothers deployed. These things would help church members to be better at reaching out to others. Encourage these as ministries and put weight on their importance.

Our pastors once helped my family and it meant a lot to them. Time is a very precious gift. Develop in congregations an attitude of a servant. Teach people to reach out and not just expect to be reached. Keep pastors from being so busy with 'church stuff', so they can spend the time with the simple stuff. Our go, go, go society has crept into the church and we need to slow down, so we can be faithful with the little things that God gives us.

Counseling is also something that I feel is very important. I have seen so many marriages fall apart as a result of the deployment process. Often, couples were seeking and open to counseling, but were shuffled from one pastor to another and never even being counseled by one. Counseling programs would help churches as well. Many couples are experiencing marital problems and solid counseling would benefit many.

Brian is also a soldier that has been on many deployments and has a few ideas on what he believes the church could do to help these that are going to be deployed and those returning:

The best thing anyone in a church or a church as a whole could do to help troops while deployed or when they return home is to get involved before the soldier ever deploys. There is a lot of red tape to get any organization onto a military base but making the effort to stay in touch with soldiers before they ever deploy is critical to the things they think about and do over seas. When they come home they know there are people who are not trying to do anything but love them. This is easier to accept when a soldier returns home if it was established before they ever left.

As one woman said to me:

Prayer, prayer and more prayer is what we military families need.

You can never pray enough for your family and friends, and if you know of a family member or have friends that are in the military, the most benefit that you can do for them is to keep them in your prayers consistently. *Everything else you do will be completely appreciated, but these military families are also needing you to pray for them.* Pray for their marriages. Pray for their children. Pray for their hearts. I am thankful for so many people for being there for me and praying for me through all of the difficult times and seasons that I sometimes muddled through. I have so many great friends who I have not mentioned in this book, and I feel like I am not giving justice to the love they have poured into me. If you are sincerely seeking to help those in the military, I pray for you that God would give you the wisdom to know what to do in each unique and difficult situation. As with everything, if it is carried forth with pure motives and a loving heart it will never be the wrong thing to do.

Tips from Chapter 14

• Pray for military families, deployed or not. Sometimes, we don't know how we can help others, and others will often not tell us or know what help they need. Pray for the Lord to direct you exactly how you can help individual soldiers, wives, children or the entire family. God will speak to us if you will listen to Him.

• If you know of a wife whose husband is deployed, ask her how you can specifically help her. If she says she's okay and doesn't need help, offer how you can specifically help her, ie. "I'll watch your kids for 3 hours on Saturday so you can get errands done or have a break" or "My teenage son will mow your lawn this weekend since he has to mow ours." Don't ask if they want it done, but just offer without it being a question.

• Invite a military family to your house for a major holiday, *especially* if the husband is deployed. Do not assume they have family to go to or that their family is close enough. Do not make them feel like they are a *project* for you, but let them feel welcomed.

Questions from Chapter 14

• Have you ever moved and been the *new kid* at school? What could people have said to you or done to make you feel more included?

• If you are a military spouse who has moved before, what needs did you have when you moved into a new location and city? When you get new neighbors who are military, new people come into your church or your children acquire new friends who are military, remember the needs that you had when you moved. Try to do all that you can to help them more easily adjust to their new location and surroundings.

• Have you been hurt by individuals or a group that you had expected to help you but didn't come through? Can you stop your mind and thoughts now and really make a concerted effort to forget them? Ephesians 4:32 tells us how important it is to forgive one another: *Be kind to one another, tenderhearted, forgiving one another, as God in Christ forgave you.* We must learn to forgive, whether we feel it or not. The fact is that we have been hurt, and forgiveness doesn't mean the hurt will go away. Realize that forgiveness is the key to our hearts' healing. When our hearts are healed, we can truly and freely love those around us .

My hope is that this book has stirred in your heart a compassion for our military families. Know that we are not wanting pity or to be patronized. We are wanting others to see that our needs are, indeed, different and unique than those in the civilian world. We want to looked at with dignity and respect, and we want our requests (either spoken or unspoken) to be known to those who would like to give us a helping hand.

POINTS YOU WANT TO REMEMBER
feel free to jot down notes below...

Nicole Brocx Lee

POINTS YOU WANT TO REMEMBER

feel free to jot down notes below...

Acknowledgements

I'd like to thank Gloria Jenney for helping to edit the first draft of this book. You have been an encouragement for such a long time, and I thank you for your interest and help.

Thank you, Robbie Grayson, for all you have done to help with *Wedding Bells.* You have helped to edit, publish (and everything else that I am not even aware of!) to get this book out of my head and into the hands of others. Your friendship throughout the years has been a tremendous blessing to me and my family, especially during an extremely difficult time in my life. You're an amazing man of God who has been a blessing to me.

I'd like to thank Greg Wark for giving me the idea to write this book in the first place and for prompting me. Thank you for your encouragement and for believing in me.

I would like to thank *all* of those who have contributed to the the writing of *Wedding Bells* with their stories and their lives. I know for many it was difficult even going back and reliving those difficult seasons of your lives. I am grateful that you entrusted me with your stories.

A special thanks goes out to by BFF (Brownie Friend Forever) Brian Shires for coming up with the name of this book and his contributions in the book,from the viewpoint of a soldier.

Last, but very importantly, I would like to thank those of you who have been praying for me both during the writing process and as this book goes out to people. You all are so very special to me: Deana Duran, Mary Cleveland, John Renken, Malachias Gaskin, Sherry Cruz, Blanca Terral, Cherie Walker, Sherry Nicholson, Barbara Wancho, Jackie Furlong, Andrew Brocx, Donald Holcomb, Andi Uffelman, Lynn Hoyt, Jill Giallanza, Jodie Carafano, Judy Weerstra, Jume Morris, Pat Barrett, and Michelle Noyes.

Nicole Brocx Lee

Another TRAITMARKER BOOK...

RALPH "MALACHIAS" GASKIN

A WARRIOR'S GARDEN

SEEDS OF A THERAPEUTIC APPROACH TO DEALING WITH POST-TRAUMATIC STRESS DISORDER (PTSD)

http://www.warriorsgarden.com/